More Planning to Teach Writing

Written by an experienced teacher and literacy consultant, *More Planning to Teach Writing* offers an easy to use, tried, and tested framework that will reduce teachers' planning time while raising standards in writing. Using the circles planning approach, it provides fresh inspiration to teachers who want to engage and enthuse their pupils, with new, exciting, and varied hooks into writing, including modern and classic picture books, short stories, and novels.

Exploring how best to use baseline assessment to build upon children's writerly knowledge and skills, each chapter puts the needs and interests of pupils at the forefront of planning and models how to design units of work that will lead to high-quality writing outcomes in any primary classroom.

The book uses a simple formula for success:

1 Find your students' gaps in learning.
2 Choose a hook that you know will engage your students.
3 Select a unit plan that you know will support you to get the best writing out of your students.
4 Tailor it to your students.
5 Teach it!

With a brand new and fantastic range of hooks to inspire teaching and learning, *More Planning to Teach Writing* ensures successful planning that will maximise engagement, enjoyment, and achievement. This book is an accessible and necessary resource for any teacher planning to teach writing in their classroom.

Emma Caulfield is an experienced literacy consultant, trainer, and teacher working in a variety of settings supporting schools to improve children's engagement, attainment, and achievement in reading and writing.

Review from Planning to Teach Writing: `This book is an accessible and necessary resource for any teacher planning to teach writing in their classroom and will be a huge help in meeting the NC requirements for writing.'

Sarah Brew, Parents in Touch

More Planning to Teach Writing

A Practical Guide for Primary School Teachers

Emma Caulfield

LONDON AND NEW YORK

First published 2021
by Routledge
2 Park Square, Milton Park, Abingdon, Oxon OX14 4RN

and by Routledge
52 Vanderbilt Avenue, New York, NY 10017

Routledge is an imprint of the Taylor & Francis Group, an informa business

© 2021 Emma Caulfield

The right of Emma Caulfield to be identified as author of this work has been asserted by her in accordance with sections 77 and 78 of the Copyright, Designs and Patents Act 1988.

All rights reserved. No part of this book may be reprinted or reproduced or utilised in any form or by any electronic, mechanical, or other means, now known or hereafter invented, including photocopying and recording, or in any information storage or retrieval system, without permission in writing from the publishers.

Trademark notice: Product or corporate names may be trademarks or registered trademarks, and are used only for identification and explanation without intent to infringe.

British Library Cataloguing-in-Publication Data
A catalogue record for this book is available from the British Library

Library of Congress Cataloging-in-Publication Data
Names: Caulfield, Emma, author.
Title: More planning to teach writing : a practical guide for primary school teachers / Emma Caulfield.
Description: Abingdon, Oxon ; New York : Routledge, 2021. | Includes bibliographical references and index.
Identifiers: LCCN 2020057600 | ISBN 9780367466084 (hardback) | ISBN 9780367466091 (paperback) | ISBN 9781003029939 (ebook)
Subjects: LCSH: Composition (Language arts)–Study and teaching (Primary) | Creative writing (Primary education) | English language–Composition and exercises–Study and teaching (Primary)
Classification: LCC LB1528 .C37 2021 | DDC 372.62/3–dc23
LC record available at https://lccn.loc.gov/2020057600

ISBN: 978-0-367-46608-4 (hbk)
ISBN: 978-0-367-46609-1 (pbk)
ISBN: 978-1-003-02993-9 (ebk)

Typeset in Helvetica Neue LT Std
by KnowledgeWorks Global Ltd

Contents

Preface ix
Introduction xi

PART 1
THE CIRCLES PLANNING APPROACH 1

PART 2
UNIT PLANS 11

CHAPTER 1
Using picture books as hooks 13

    KEY STAGE 1: MIND MAPS AND UNIT PLANS 15

  Amazing Grace **by Mary Hoffman** 16
    Unit plans: Information Page, Narrative, Persuasion 17

  Journey **by Aaron Becker** 20
    Unit plans: Explanation, Narrative, Recount 21

  Naughty Bus **by Jan and Jerry Oke** 24
    Unit plans: Instructions, Narrative, Persuasion 25

  One Snowy Night **by Nick Butterworth** 28
    Unit plans: Information Page, Narrative, Recount 29

***Stick Man* by Julia Donaldson and Axel Scheffler** — 32
    Unit plans: Information, Instructions, Narrative — 33

***Tad* by Benji Davies** — 36
    Unit plans: Description, Explanation, Narrative — 37

***The Day the Crayons Quit* by Drew Daywalt and Oliver Jeffers** — 40
    Unit plans: Narrative, Persuasion, Recount — 41

***The Disgusting Sandwich* by Gareth Edwards and Hannah Shaw** — 44
    Unit plans: Instructions, Narrative, Recount — 45

***The Lighthouse Keeper's Lunch* by Ronda and David Armitage** — 48
    Unit plans: Description, Explanation, Narrative — 49

***The Tear Thief* by Carol Ann Duffy and Nicoletta Ceccoli** — 52
    Unit plans: Description, Instructions, Narrative — 53

***The Tiger Who Came to Tea* by Judith Kerr** — 56
    Unit plans: Invitation & Menu, Narrative, Recount — 57

***The Way Back Home* by Oliver Jeffers** — 60
    Unit plans: Information Page, Narrative, Persuasion — 61

KEY STAGE 2: MIND MAPS AND UNIT PLANS — 65

***Ahmed and the Feather Girl* by Jane Ray** — 66
    Unit plans: Instructions, Narrative, News Report — 67

***Pandora* by Victoria Turnbull** — 70
    Unit plans: Setting Description, Instructions, Narrative — 71

***Quest* by Aaron Becker** — 74
    Unit plans: Explanation, Instructions, Narrative

***Sir Lancelot's First Quest from King Arthur and the Knights of the Round Table* Retold by Marcia Williams** — 78
    Unit plans: Discussion, Narrative, Persuasion — 79

***Storm Whale* by Sarah Brennan** — 82
    Unit plans: Description & Action, Discussion, Narrative — 83

***The Dark* by Lemony Snicket** — 86
    Unit plans: Explanation, Information, Narrative — 87

***The Egg* by M.P. Robertson** — 90
    Unit plans: Explanation, Narrative, Recount Letter — 91

***The Elephant's Friend* Retold by Marcia Williams** — 94
    Unit plans: Information Text, Narrative, Persuasion — 95

***The Ice Bear* by Jackie Morris** — 98
    Unit plans: Information, Narrative, Persuasion — 99

***The Tin Forest* by Helen Ward and Wayne Anderson** — 102
    Unit plans: Narrative, Persuasion, Recount (diary) — 103

***The True Story of the 3 Little Pigs* by Jon Scieszka**	**106**
Unit plans: Discussion, Information, Narrative	107

CHAPTER 2
Using novels and short stories as hooks **111**

KEY STAGE 1: MIND MAPS AND UNIT PLANS	**113**
Great Sharp Scissors* by Philippa Pearce	**114**
Unit plans: Narrative, Persuasion (Advert), Recount	115
Lion at School* by Philippa Pearce	**118**
Unit plans: Description, Explanation, Narrative	119
Little Lord Feather-Frock* Retold by Hugh Lupton	**122**
Unit plans: Narrative, Persuasion, Recount	123
***Mr Majeika* by Humphrey Carpenter**	**126**
Unit plans: Explanation, Instructions, Narrative	127
Mrs Pepperpot has a visitor from America* by Alf Prøysen	**130**
Unit plans: Information, Narrative, Persuasion	131
Mrs Pepperpot's Birthday* by Alf Prøysen	**134**
Unit plans: Information Page, Instructions, Narrative	135
***Peter and the Wolf* by Sergei Prokofiev**	**138**
Unit plans: Explanation, Information, Narrative	139
Rumpelstiltskin* Retold by Philip Pullman	**142**
Unit plans: Narrative, Recount, Persuasion	143
The Blue Coat* Retold by Hugh Lupton	**146**
Unit plans: Information, Instructions, Narrative	147
***The Enchanted Wood* by Enid Blyton**	**150**
Unit plans: Explanation, Information Page, Narrative	151
***The Twits* by Roald Dahl**	**154**
Unit plans: Information, Instructions, Narrative	155

Denotes a short story from an anthology

KEY STAGE 2: MIND MAPS AND UNIT PLANS	**159**
The Brave Little Tailor* Retold by Philip Pullman	**160**
Unit plans: Discussion, Explanation, Narrative	161
***Cogheart* by Peter Bunzl**	**164**
Unit plans: Character & Setting Descriptions, Explanation, Narrative	165
The Donkey Cabbage* Retold by Philip Pullman	**168**
Unit plans: Instructions, Narrative, Persuasion	169

***Fireweed* by Jill Paton Walsh** — **172**
 Unit plans: Setting Descriptions, Narrative, Recount (Letter) — 173

Grandpa's Story* by Shaun Tan — **176**
 Unit plans: Narrative, Persuasion, Recount — 177

***Letters from the Lighthouse* by Emma Carroll** — **180**
 Unit plans: Information, Narrative, Recount — 181

Mackerel and Chips* by Michael Morpurgo — **184**
 Unit plans: Information, Narrative, Persuasion — 185

The Balaclava Story* by George Layton — **188**
 Unit plans: Discussion, Information, Narrative — 189

***The Girl of Ink and Stars* by Kiran Millwood Hargrave** — **192**
 Unit plans: Narrative, Persuasion, News Report — 193

The Grendel* by Anthony Horowitz — **196**
 Unit plans: Description & Action, Discussion, Narrative — 197

***The Legend of Podkin One-Ear* by Kieran Larwood** — **200**
 Unit plans: Recount (Biography), Information, Narrative — 201

***The Tale of Despereaux* by Kate DiCamillo** — **204**
 Unit plans: Discussion, Instructions, Narrative — 205

Undertow* by Shaun Tan — **208**
 Unit plans: Explanation, Narrative, News Report — 209

***Varjak Paw* by SF Said** — **212**
 Unit plans: Information, Narrative, Persuasion — 213

*Denotes a short story from an anthology

References — 217
Appendix — 219
Index — 225

Preface

This book will help teachers to produce effective unit plans for writing, and in doing so, they will be able to concentrate on the core business of teaching units that help children to fulfil their potential as writers.

I have been in Education since 1990 when I started my teaching degree at Liverpool Hope University (was L.I.H.E.). That year an inspirational English tutor, Jean Clarkson, put us into pairs and asked us to read picture books with one another. That was the beginning of my love affair with picture books. Ever since that day, I have used books to inspire learners over and over again.

The visual image and how it can be used to inspire and engage children became the focus of my Master's thesis (in 2005); this time it was in the form of films and pictures. My research told me that using visual images to stimulate writing engaged almost all writers, and in particular, lower achieving writers.

By then, I was a Literacy Consultant working solely to support primary schools in their plight to improve achievement in reading and writing. I discovered that whilst many teachers knew what would engage learners, they did not know how to use the hooks within a broader teaching sequence.

In response to this, I developed tools and training packages to support teachers with planning sequences of work that led to rapid and sustained improvement in the writing achievement of pupils. However, in many cases, these sequences were not having the impact that they should as teachers were not focussed enough, in the initial planning stages, on what their pupils needed to improve on. It was clear that brilliant teaching was not leading to successful learning.

So, by bringing the elements of the well-known cycle of 'assess, plan, teach, assess' together, I found that writing achievement improved rapidly. It was necessary to spend time supporting teachers in both assessment and planning; the more I did, the more I realised that it wasn't rocket science and everyone should know how to do this. Vitally, in addition to raising standards of achievement, this approach was cutting teacher' workload.

It is a fact that there is a direct correlation between standards of literacy and quality and longevity of adult life. The primary school teacher's role within this cannot and should not be underestimated; I hope that this book will help them to inspire and engage learners so that they can become the best possible writers.

Introduction

> Effective composition involves articulating and communicating ideas, and then organising them coherently for a reader. This requires clarity, awareness of the audience, purpose and context and an increasingly wide knowledge of vocabulary and grammar. Writing also depends on fluent, legible and, eventually speedy handwriting.
>
> (National Curriculum in England, DfE, 2013)

The curriculum gives us a framework to follow – a guide to what we, as teachers in the classroom in England, are required to teach. Often the curriculum is divided up, for example, by year group, or by theme – composition, spelling, handwriting, etc., but teachers *have* to use their professional knowledge and skills to decide what, within the curriculum, their pupils can already do and what they already know, and what they still need to learn. Without this, the teacher will be covering the curriculum, but not actually teaching it.

Figure 1 demonstrates how the curriculum and the teacher's knowledge of the pupils' learning come together, with knowledge of pedagogy, to create the optimum pedagogic approach. It is my belief that without 'knowledge of child', the teacher is likely to have little impact on learning. One area within this knowledge is where the child is up to in his or her learning.

Assessment is the key tool that teachers use to help them to decide where pupils are up to. The summative assessments (Assessment *of* Learning) check how much and what learning has taken place after a period of teaching whereas the formative assessments (Assessment *for* Learning) provide an on-going, often daily picture of where pupils' learning is up to. In 2002 the Assessment Reform Group said that 'Assessment for learning is fundamental to the development of independent learners…the process of seeking and interpreting evidence for use by learners and their teachers to decide where the learners are in their learning, where they need to go and how best to get there'.

I fundamentally and absolutely agree that Assessment for Learning is an essential part of a teacher's daily work. Always thinking 'has the pupil understood that?' and 'where does the pupil need to go next?' and 'do I need to go back over that again for pupil x or y?' However, when it comes to teaching writing, exclusively using Assessment for Learning to drive teaching, can

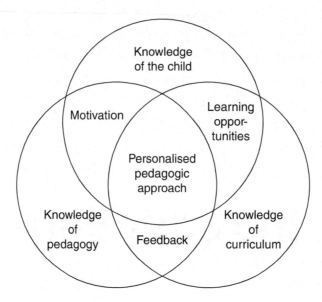

Figure 1 Combined knowledge needed to personalise learning in a classroom
Source: Dudley P. (2011)

lead to teaching being reactive and fragmented. This means that planned units of work skim the surface of learning without embedding it; for example, they may teach children about the use of longer sentences for description without progressing them as writers by addressing a specific learning point, for individual pupils or groups of pupils, within 'long sentences'.

To take the example further, during teaching of a narrative unit, I may mark the children's drafts and find that many children are not using their punctuation accurately. I make a mental note to do some more teaching about punctuation within the next unit, or I may even put the teaching sequence for narrative writing on hold and spend a couple of sessions on punctuation. Hence, as a teacher, I am reacting to issues as they emerge, and fragmenting the teaching of the narrative unit by dropping in other bits.

The premise of this book is that a teacher's summative assessment of pupils' writing is what should drive their planning. They should plan each unit of work based on a summative assessment; this assessment should be relevant to both the text type and children as writers. In doing so, the teacher strategically plans units of work; being pro-active as opposed to reactive. Of course, once teaching those units, the teacher will be using the information gathered on a daily basis to tweak teaching or address misconceptions, nevertheless it is the summative assessment that drives the teaching.

Considering Figure 1 and 'knowledge of child', I have discussed the learning needs of pupils vis-a-vis writing, and will expand on this shortly; however, it is also important to remember that it is essential to tap into the interests of pupils in order to truly engage them in writing. 'We write best about what we know and what matters' Pie Corbett (Talk for Writing). In order to find out what children know about and what matters to them, we need to get to know more about our pupils than simply how they perform in tasks. Additionally, once we know what interests them, it is also important to set up genuinely meaningful writing opportunities.

> Pupils' experience in English extended beyond the classroom. They did this first through the provision of rich extra-curricular experiences outside school.... Classroom activities involved real tasks, purposes, audiences and issues related to the local or wider community. In this way, the curriculum matched pupils' needs and interests.
>
> (Ofsted 2011)

Gathering assessment information: finding the gaps

As a starting point, you will need some robust assessments of your pupils as writers – regardless of what system you are using to record your assessments, the following process relies on the teacher having a clear record of what each pupil can do in writing, and therefore, highlighting what they need to develop or learn next. Your assessment system will reflect the writing curriculum as you will be measuring achievement against curriculum expectations.

I suggest that gaps in writing are identified in three discrete areas: (1) words and language, (2) text structure, and (3) sentence structure and punctuation. For later-stage emergent writers or children who are beginning to write sentences, it would be better to leave the text structure focus and put more energies into the other two aspects, or only have two aspects.

Although there are, of course, generic writing skills, there are also skills that are specific to a text type. For example, the use of dialogue may be limited to narrative writing; the use of organisational devices is specific to non-fiction texts. For planning to address specific as well as generic skills, summative assessments can be carried out before the unit is planned.

Many people know these assessments as 'cold writes'; these tasks can be disastrous if they make children feel uncomfortable or unhappy about writing. If children feel this way, their confidence as independent writers will be eroded *and* the writing will not show the child in the best light. Therefore, it is vital that these assessment tasks be designed so that children feel comfortable and have plenty of ideas to put in writing. For example, if you are going to be teaching a story with dialogue, the task for assessment could be to write a short piece of dialogue. The stimulus might be a photograph of three characters having a heated discussion or an illustration from a picture book. A non-fiction assessment example for writing an information text might be to ask children to write an information text about your school for a new child.

Work back from what the final writing outcome is going to be in order to think about what the baseline writing needs to show you. This will help you to formulate a task that yields some writing that can then inform your plan. Taking the above non-fiction example further, if the final outcome is an information text with distinct paragraphs, then it is likely that you will be looking in the baseline writings, not only for paragraphs but also for cohesion within and between paragraphs. Paragraphing will give you the text structure target, cohesive devices will be the sentence structure target, and the language of cohesion will be the words and language target.

Now, you have your three main targets for the class; they will be differentiated according to the needs of your various attainment groups.

For example,

Whole class targets:

1 Use synonyms for said
2 Vary paragraph openers
3 Use correct speech punctuation

Differentiation:

1 Use synonyms for said – lower writers
  Use synonyms for said effectively – middle and high writers
2 Group ideas into paragraphs – lower writers
  Vary paragraph openers – middle writers
  Use effective paragraph openers – high writers
3 Use inverted commas correctly – lower writers
  Use correct speech punctuation – middle and high writers

You can easily assess progress in each of these targets through the children's final independent piece of writing.

Plugging the gaps

Once you know what you need to teach, you are one-third of the way there. Planning a teaching sequence that leads to improvement in writing (both plugging of gaps and consolidation of skills) is the next step, and, of course, teaching is the final stage.

You can then use your assessment of how successful the pieces of writing are, combined with target progress to inform the teaching of your next unit/s.

Finally

Through using exciting and varied hooks into writing, this book provides inspiration for teachers who want to engage and enthuse their pupils. For each hook, there are suggestions of four different text types – these are in the form of mind-maps – and three worked unit plans.

To get the best out of this book, follow these simple steps:

1. Find the gaps in learning for your students (as set out above).
2. Choose a hook (picture book, short story or novel) that you know will engage your students.
3. Select a unit plan that you know will support you to get the best writing out of your students.
4. Tailor it (add direct teaching elements that are needed).
5. Teach.
6. Assess and evaluate the success of the unit.

When you have used a few of these mind-maps and plans, you can begin to create your own using the templates provided.

The circles planning approach

The approach to medium-term planning used in this book is centred on a model provided by the Primary National Strategies (PNS). This model is taken from Eve Bearne's excellently researched structure for planning as set out in the joint UKLA/PNS publication 'Raising Boys' Achievements in Writing' (2004). Longer, extended units of work are planned following a sequence of first reading, then planning, and, finally, writing.

> Based on the work of Bearne (2002), the research recommended a structured sequence to planning where the children and teachers began by familiarising themselves with a text type, capturing ideas for their own writing followed by scaffolded writing experiences, resulting in independent written outcomes.
>
> (PNS 2008)

Not only does this approach allow teachers to see the big picture of a unit before they start teaching, it also enables them to plan a rich and impactful learning journey. Additionally, as the broad view of teaching is clear in the teacher's head, s/he is better equipped to allow the unit to twist and turn according to the needs and interests of learners. The research findings in 2004 were:

> …a three-week block was a new way of working, which was challenging but was seen to reap considerable benefit. For example:
> …the slow build up to the writing objective really helped my young writers, particularly the boys who enjoyed the variety across time around one text.
> …identifying specific long term intentions for each unit…enabled them to work more flexibly
> and creatively as they travelled towards these intentions and prompted them to listen to the children more acutely in the process. In focusing on the writing end product, they

explicitly 'built in more time to develop thinking and imagination' and 'planned for more time for the children to enact and perform'.

...a general sense of satisfaction in being able to cover short-term objectives within a longer

time frame. Some felt that in the past, in trying to cover a range of short-term objectives, their work had been fragmented; they enjoyed what they perceived as increased flexibility to respond to the needs and interests of the children, whilst still being guided by the overall intention of the unit.

(UKLA/PNS 2004)

The strongest and the most structured parts of my recommended model are the first two phases: the teaching and learning that build up to the children drafting and shaping their writing. Once these parts are taught, the teacher will have a greater sense of how long they need to give to the shared, guided, and supported part of 'the final write'. If the ground work has been done, children will have firm foundations upon which to build – they will find the writing easier and more successful. The UKLA/PNS (2004) study called this 'Providing time to journey'; it found that

A core issue emerged of a focus on less literal time allocated to writing, but more generative thinking time in the form of an extended enquiry through drama and visual approaches. This time was energetically spent in imaginative and engaging explorations of texts. Such time was significant as it allowed the teachers/practitioners to feel less hurried and to listen and learn more about individuals. It also meant that when the children did undertake writing, they were unusually focused and sustained their commitment, persisting and completing their work.

The third phase of teaching and learning should also be mapped out so that the teacher has a sense of how the writing will progress over time. Two considerations may be whether they will ask children to write in chunks, using teacher modelling to support as and when needed or whether they will be drafting in one sitting and following it up with some redrafting over time. What we know is that providing space and time for children to develop a piece of writing leads to better quality writing:

Allowing time for the writing to develop and giving the learners space in which to develop their ideas and move slowly and gradually towards a final piece of writing...clearly influenced the quality of the final pieces and partly accounted for the raised standards in writing.

(UKLA/PNS 2004)

Independent writing

The circles planning approach assumes that children are given opportunities to independently use and apply their writing skills at the end of the three phases. Teachers must provide opportunities for children to show what they have learned and to practise writing entirely independently. Following any non-fiction unit, children should have the opportunity to use and apply their skills across the curriculum. Additionally, children should be required to independently write short (or long) narratives once they are confident of story writing.

Gathering assessment information: finding the gaps

As a starting point, you will need some robust assessments of your pupils as writers – regardless of what system you are using to record your assessments, the following process relies on the teacher having a clear record of what each pupil can do in writing, and therefore, highlighting what they need to develop or learn next. Your assessment system will reflect the writing curriculum as you will be measuring achievement against curriculum expectations.

I suggest that gaps in writing are identified in three discrete areas: (1) words and language, (2) text structure, and (3) sentence structure and punctuation. For later-stage emergent writers or children who are beginning to write sentences, it would be better to leave the text structure focus and put more energies into the other two aspects, or only have two aspects.

Although there are, of course, generic writing skills, there are also skills that are specific to a text type. For example, the use of dialogue may be limited to narrative writing; the use of organisational devices is specific to non-fiction texts. For planning to address specific as well as generic skills, summative assessments can be carried out before the unit is planned.

Many people know these assessments as 'cold writes'; these tasks can be disastrous if they make children feel uncomfortable or unhappy about writing. If children feel this way, their confidence as independent writers will be eroded *and* the writing will not show the child in the best light. Therefore, it is vital that these assessment tasks be designed so that children feel comfortable and have plenty of ideas to put in writing. For example, if you are going to be teaching a story with dialogue, the task for assessment could be to write a short piece of dialogue. The stimulus might be a photograph of three characters having a heated discussion or an illustration from a picture book. A non-fiction assessment example for writing an information text might be to ask children to write an information text about your school for a new child.

Work back from what the final writing outcome is going to be in order to think about what the baseline writing needs to show you. This will help you to formulate a task that yields some writing that can then inform your plan. Taking the above non-fiction example further, if the final outcome is an information text with distinct paragraphs, then it is likely that you will be looking in the baseline writings, not only for paragraphs but also for cohesion within and between paragraphs. Paragraphing will give you the text structure target, cohesive devices will be the sentence structure target, and the language of cohesion will be the words and language target.

Now, you have your three main targets for the class; they will be differentiated according to the needs of your various attainment groups.

For example,

Whole class targets:

1. Use synonyms for said
2. Vary paragraph openers
3. Use correct speech punctuation

Differentiation:

1. Use synonyms for said – lower writers
   Use synonyms for said effectively – middle and high writers
2. Group ideas into paragraphs – lower writers
   Vary paragraph openers – middle writers
   Use effective paragraph openers – high writers
3. Use inverted commas correctly – lower writers
   Use correct speech punctuation – middle and high writers

You can easily assess progress in each of these targets through the children's final independent piece of writing.

Plugging the gaps

Once you know what you need to teach, you are one-third of the way there. Planning a teaching sequence that leads to improvement in writing (both plugging of gaps and consolidation of skills) is the next step, and, of course, teaching is the final stage.

You can then use your assessment of how successful the pieces of writing are, combined with target progress to inform the teaching of your next unit/s.

Finally

Through using exciting and varied hooks into writing, this book provides inspiration for teachers who want to engage and enthuse their pupils. For each hook, there are suggestions of four different text types – these are in the form of mind-maps – and three worked unit plans.

To get the best out of this book, follow these simple steps:

1 Find the gaps in learning for your students (as set out above).
2 Choose a hook (picture book, short story or novel) that you know will engage your students.
3 Select a unit plan that you know will support you to get the best writing out of your students.
4 Tailor it (add direct teaching elements that are needed).
5 Teach.
6 Assess and evaluate the success of the unit.

When you have used a few of these mind-maps and plans, you can begin to create your own using the templates provided.

TEACHING SEQUENCE FOR WRITING

PHASE 1
Immersion in text
Shared reading
Enjoy, explore and respond to text
Develop comprehension skills
Identify language/genre features
Collect writer's hints and vocabulary

PHASE 2
Gather ideas
Oral rehearsal
Plan

PHASE 3
Shared writing
Teacher modelling
Teacher scribing
Supported composition
Guided writing
Independent writing
Draft, revise, edit

Independent writing task

In most primary schools there are long-term plans for the writing curriculum, which record the coverage and content for each term of the year; there are medium-term plans, which indicate the coverage and content for each block of work, or 'unit'; and there are daily plans.

Each circles plan covers what has come to be known as a unit of work. The timescale for coverage of the unit depends on the amount of teaching and learning that needs to be done, and on the pace at which pupils learn. For example, a poetry unit on creating shape poems may span five lessons, or a narrative unit on creating a spooky story may span fifteen lessons. Broadly, before the unit starts, the teacher will have a sense of how many lessons it will take for children to complete the journey through the phases of learning; however, there must be flexibility so that if pupils need parts of the journey to be repeated or skipped, then this should happen.

The circles plan is made up of three phases. Each phase plays an equal and vital part in building up to a final written outcome. Progression through the phases should feel like a journey for both pupils and teachers – a teaching journey for teachers and a learning journey for pupils. The journey should have twists and turns; there may even be diversions and delays, but the process itself should be enriching and engaging, and the final outcome: the destination should be truly fulfilling.

The purpose of phase 1 is for the pupils to be fully immersed in a text – the text type that they will eventually be authors of. The final outcome of phase 1 should always be that pupils know 'what a good one looks like' (WAGOLL), and in many cases, 'sounds like' too. Phase 2 is the time for pupils to think about, plan, orally rehearse, and play with their ideas for writing. Phase 3 is the writing phase; an opportunity for children to be *taught* how to bring everything together into a successful piece of writing. The journey begins at reading and ends with writing. This process is also known as (and rooted in) the 'Teaching Sequence for Writing'.

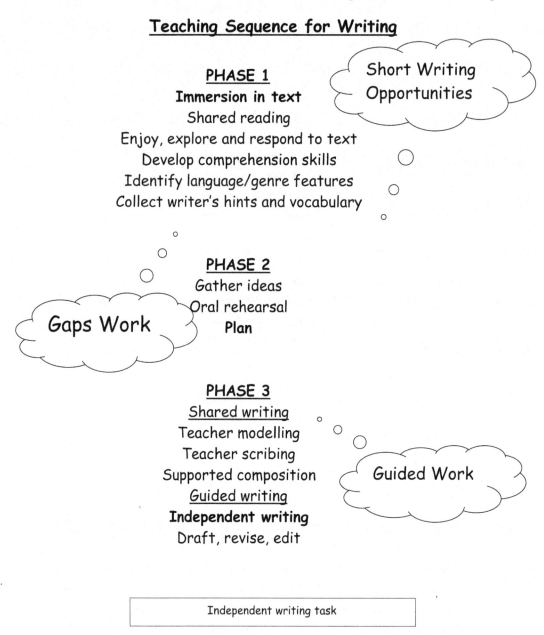

We have already established that the Teaching Sequence for Writing has three phases that are discrete yet linked, which is why it is presented as a Venn diagram. We also know that the sequence is a map that guides teaching through a journey, the final destination of which is a piece of writing. The sequence is just that – a guide – it is the big picture of a unit of work; it should not be followed to the letter (the detail of teaching will be in the daily planning), but flex in response to pupils' learning. Equally, there are no timescales attached to the sequence. Some units may take a week of lessons; others may take three weeks.

Phase 1: immersion in text type

AIM OF PHASE 1: TO KNOW WHAT A GOOD ONE LOOKS AND SOUNDS LIKE

A simple fact that cannot be argued with is that it is very difficult to write a particular text type if you are not familiar with it. Familiarisation with the text type is the first step; by the end of phase 1, children should be so immersed in it that they could write it if they had to. In *The Really Useful Literacy Book*, Martin et al. (2004: 39–41) say that:

> writers have to have read the text type they are trying to write or have it read to them... From the experience of being read to and then wide reading, the writer builds ideas of what a successful piece of writing looks and sounds like...Children need to read and read and read – in order to both absorb the structures, sentence constructions and vocabulary of written texts...

Immersion is done through shared reading, when the teacher acts as a model reader making overt what good readers do, for example, by paying attention to the punctuation, using expression and intonation to aid understanding and bring the text alive, and asking themselves questions and predicting. Pupils should always be able to see and follow the text during shared reading.

Shared reading is an opportunity to examine the purpose and audience of text, as this will be very useful when pupils begin to write their own: 'if we add together purpose and audience (why am I writing and who will be reading it?) we find ourselves considering the best ways to construct the text we want to write' (Martin et al. 2004: 34).

In addition to and during shared reading, the text should be brought alive so that children engage with it, understand it and respond to it as readers. It is really important that children are given opportunities to explore their responses to text; as children engage in 'booktalk', an expression coined by Aidan Chambers (1993) in his 'Tell Me' approach. They experience being the audience – understand how it feels to make sense of, and respond emotionally to what they read. The purpose of this, within the teaching sequence for writing, is to help writers to begin to consider what response they may want to elicit from the reader. You can't truly write for an audience unless you've walked in the footsteps of the audience.

Besides eliciting the reader's response, immersion in the text enables children to hear and collect vocabulary and language patterns, internalise plot structures, and deepen their understanding. At this point in phase 1, children should be supported to gather vocabulary that they like and think they will utilise in their writing, and appropriate synonyms too.

Equally, rather than the teacher giving the children a list of elements that feature in a text type, they should be collecting them as they read and engage in the text type. During phase 1, children should be given opportunities to collect, in addition to vocabulary, ideas and authorial effects to be used, later, in their own compositions. These lists are sometimes referred to as 'success criteria' or similar; however, it is my belief that the more child-friendly, less threatening labels such as 'writer's hints' make more sense to children, and therefore, are more likely to be used when they write. These lists can be used as checklists during or after writing, but they should always be displayed, perhaps on a 'working wall', during the unit.

Booktalk and close analysis of the text – this time focussing on *how* the writer has achieved effects on the reader, and being supported to understand what the writer has done to elicit this response and have that effect – are also key parts of phase 1 of the teaching sequence. These ideas should be added to the 'writer's hints' list mentioned above.

Phase 2: gathering ideas and shaping them into a plan

AIM OF PHASE 2: TO HAVE PLANNED MY WRITING

In order to be ready to compose a text, we need to have collected ideas, played with them, decided on the best ones and then shaped them into some form of a plan. This is what phase 2 is for.

Initially, experimentation is the key – children should be freed up so that the ideas flow. They should be encouraged to share ideas; identify what might work; play with vocabulary and language so that they can find the best way to express themselves; and orally rehearse. All of these methods involve talk. Fisher et al. (2010: 39) state that 'talk will help them think up and extend their ideas but also…help them to gain a better understanding of the writing task set by the teacher'. Ros Fisher explores using talk to generate ideas through role-play, drawing on experience, using pictures and artefacts, and telling others.

In his Talk for Writing approach, Pie Corbett (2008: 6–7) suggests the use of:

- Writer-talk games…to develop and focus aspects of ideas and language for writing
- Word and language games to stimulate the imagination and develop vocabulary and the use of language
- Role play and drama to explore ideas, themes, and aspects of the developing writing

Once children have had opportunities to talk through their ideas, they should then be shaped into a plan. This may be a story map, mountain or a story board, a series of boxes or a skeleton. It is my opinion that schools should have set planning pro-forma so that pupils become familiar with the format; I also believe that planning formats should be the same for all text types.

Phase 3: extended write/completion of whole text

AIM OF PHASE 3: TO HAVE DRAFTED AND REFINED A PIECE OF WRITING

Once children 'know' the text type (from phase 1) and have planned their own (in phase 2), they should be ready to write. The first step of phase 3 is to support the children to get started on their writing through shared writing. Shared and guided writing are the only opportunities a teacher has to truly teach writing. Shared writing has three elements: teacher modelling, teacher scribing, and supported composition.

When a teacher models writing, s/he demonstrates and makes explicit what a writer does when s/he composes. As s/he goes on narrating, the teacher shows pupils how to write; how to use the plan and writer's hints to support with structuring the writing and ideas; and how to orally rehearse sentences, re-read, and edit 'on the run'. Acting as a scribe in 'teacher scribing', the teacher takes ideas from the children and shapes them into a piece of writing. S/he does this by enabling pupils to focus on the texts they have been immersed in, the writer's hints, and the plan; helping them to generate ideas and selecting the most appropriate or powerful; and balancing their 'expert' skills with the pupils' developing knowledge to produce a good quality written piece.

'Supported composition' can act as the bridge between modelled writing and independent writing. It provides pupils with an opportunity to 'have a go' on mini-whiteboards (or similar) whilst in a supportive environment. During supported composition, the teacher supports writers by providing the stimulus and challenge and picking up on misconceptions, whilst the pupils write. Often pupils only write a little bit – perhaps a sentence or two – then they share and refine their writing and take it away with them as a starting point.

Shared writing is usually carried out as a whole-class activity. Small group work or 'guided writing' is another feature of phase 3 (although guided work should also be woven through phases 1 and 2). This is the time for a teacher to work with a small group on a specific aspect of its writing; it may be around sentence or paragraph development, or language use, or it may have a broader focus such as text structure or editing. The importance of taking the time to work with small groups cannot be over-emphasised. For many busy primary practitioners, this is really the *only* time that pupils are taught specific writing skills in a targeted way – done well; it has the most powerful impact on the quality of children's writing.

Independent writing can and should only be expected from pupils once they have been equipped with the skills and knowledge needed to do so successfully. Many teachers wonder and debate with colleagues how independent a final piece is if pupils have been given support in writing it. To me, this is simply 'teaching'! If I give children the knowledge, skills, and confidence to write independently, and they go off and write independently (using some of the ideas and strategies as support), then they are indeed 'independent' writers.

The final part of any 'good' writing is checking and editing. The National Curriculum in England 2013 (Department for Education, 2013) states that it is an end of KS2 requirement for children to be able to:

Evaluate and edit [writing] by:

- assessing the effectiveness of their own and others' writing and suggesting improvements
- proposing changes to grammar and vocabulary to improve consistency, including the accurate use of pronouns in sentences
- proofreading for spelling and punctuation errors
- reading aloud their own writing, to a group or the whole class, using appropriate intonation and controlling the tone and volume so that the meaning is clear.

Polishing writing to ensure that it communicates exactly what and how the writer intends is a vital skill for children to be taught, regardless of these statutory elements; therefore, it should always be included in phase 3.

Other elements that are woven through the phases

In addition to, and integral to, the teaching content of the three phases, there are short writes, guided group work, and gaps (target) teaching. All of these are a fundamental part of the teaching sequence; without them, the quality of the final written outcomes and subsequent attempts at the same text type may be disappointing, as learning will not be deep enough.

Throughout phases 1 and 2, short writing opportunities should be planned. These may vary in length from writing up new vocabulary into journals through to paragraphs of information or narrative. Short writes keep children writing! They allow children to practise what they have been taught, record ideas, and exercise their writing muscles.

The benefits of guided writing have already been mentioned. Once the activities for the phases are planned, the teacher should identify a group to work with during each activity. The focus of the session will depend on the children in the group and what they need; for example, during phase 1, a group may need support for using effective vocabulary (that they have collected) or for a specific sentence level issue; during phase 2, they may need support for creating a plan, or preparing questions for hot-seating.

Finally, gaps teaching needs to be identified during the phases and planned for. Direct teaching may be done in discrete slots followed by opportunities to practise new skills and knowledge during the unit of work. For example, if children need to be able to use commas to mark clauses, during phase 1, they might be identifying commas and discussing the 'job' that they do in sentences. Then, the teacher may directly teach about commas to mark clauses. This would be followed by some sentence games to practise the new knowledge.

In phase 2, the teacher may plan some more practise activities so that children can 'play' with commas to mark clauses, and then in phase 3, s/he can ensure that the use of commas to mark clauses is demonstrated during shared writing.

The hook

The best tool that a teacher has in his/her toolkit is the one that hooks the children into writing. Once engaged, children want to write and they write well. In her blog about the use of video, drama, and real-life experience as hooks into writing, Parietti (2013) said '…using these [ideas and approaches] as hooks and new ways to stimulate the children, gets them excited in a lesson and it's this excitement and engagement that means they'll achieve the most'.

Powerful texts (novels, short stories, poems, comic-strip, and picture books) can all provide superb hooks into writing. 'If…we use powerful texts as the basis of our literacy teaching, we stand the best chance of motivating children to undertake the work' (Martin et al. 2004: 12). They go on to say that 'In their research in London with Year 5 children published as 'The Reader in the Writer' (2001), Myra Barrs and Valerie Cork…suggest that the reading of powerful texts was one of the key factors responsible for children producing high quality writing'. (Martin et al. 2004: 12).

A hook can be used right at the start of a unit, or it may be better to put it in the end of phase 1 – once the pupils have been immersed in the text type – so as to stimulate ideas in phase 2. For example, if children are going to write their own versions of the David Wiesner story 'Tuesday' (which is about frogs flying!), the hook could go at the start: a trail of lily pads could be dotted about the classroom. If they are going to write newspaper reports about flying frogs, then the hook could go after phase 1 (when they are familiar with the newspaper report text type) in the form of the book being shared.

Hooks can be huge and exciting or small and enticing. It is up to the teacher to plan the right hook for the children, and indeed, the text type.

Model texts

When it's a short story, a hook can act as a model text. However, most of the hooks in this book are either too long or not appropriate to act as both hook and model. A model text needs to be one that helps the teacher to teach the children the art of writing a particular text type, for example, *The Day the Crayons Quit* by Drew Daywalt and Oliver Jeffers provides a model of letter writing, but not of a particular story. Kiran Millwood Hargrave's (2016) novel *The Girl of Ink and Stars* provides models of many aspects of narrative writing such as characterisation and dialogue, but is not a model of a short story.

Most of the planning in this book suggests that the teacher uses a model to teach plot, structure, format, and features during phase 1 as opposed to, or in addition to, the hook.

Independent writing

When the three phases are completed, I recommend that children are provided with an opportunity to use and apply their writing skills in an independent writing task. For narrative writing, you may want to wait a few weeks before asking the children to write a story independently. The task should be interesting and exciting; it should generate writing that shows the children at their best. Ensure that children have a chance to discuss their ideas and plan their writing before they begin, and be careful that they aren't rushed through the task. Plan to do the writing task when there is a good amount of time, and do it at a time that works well for your young writers, for example, don't choose a Friday afternoon or a slot when the class usually does Physical Education (PE) sport or art!

Finally, ensure that children proofread their writing and correct errors and edit the writing if necessary, before the independent writing task finishes. Teachers will have taught them how to do this during phase 3 so they should expect children to use and apply these skills too.

How to complete a circles plan

Naturally, you have two starting points of a unit plan. One is to know what text type you are going to teach, and the other is to know what knowledge and skills you are going to teach in order to improve the children's writing. Be careful, if the text type you have chosen does not help you to teach the parts that will improve your pupils' writing, change the text type!

1. Start by planning the final outcome (what you want the children to produce at the end of the unit), what will it be? Be specific, for example, 'an information page for a class book' is better than 'an information text'. Now, add onto it what knowledge/skills you are looking to develop through the text type, for example, well-structured paragraphs or effective use of inverted commas for dialogue or use of commas to mark clauses (this knowledge or skills will be related to the 'gap' targets). If you do this, your final outcome should always be:
   - To write a ⬚specific text type goes here⬚ with ⬚two specific writing knowledge/skills to be improved go here⬚.

   For example, write an information leaflet with a clear structure and technical vocabulary. The areas to develop are generic for the class; later when you come to complete your daily plans, you will need to consider how these will be differentiated.

2. Complete the 'targets' boxes for each phase. This remains the same for all three phases – it is the key areas that you are focussing on throughout the unit. The example here is 'clear structure and technical vocabulary'.

3. Plan the outcome for the end of phase 1. As the purpose of phase 1 is to immerse the pupils in the text type so that they know what a good one looks and sounds like, the outcome will be:
   - To know what a good ⬚specific text type goes here⬚ looks and sounds like.

4. Plan the outcome for end of phase 2. As the purpose of phase 2 is to prepare the children for writing their own composition, the outcome will be:
   - I have planned my ⬚specific text type goes here⬚.

5. List the activities that you would like to use to teach the aspects needed in phases 1, 2, and 3. Be as specific as you can, for example, 'shared read three information leaflets on...' or name the text and page numbers that you will share. In phase 2, 'hot-seat the zoo keeper to find out...'. For phase 3, you need to map out how you think the shared/guided/independent writing will go (this may change as you teach it, to flex with the children as their written outcomes evolve).

6. Go through your activities and check that you have put 'target' teaching and practice activities into each phase – remember that it is this teaching that will truly move your pupils' writing forward.

7. Go through the phases 1 and 2 activities and check that you have included short writing opportunities.

10 THE CIRCLES PLANNING APPROACH

8 Consider audience and purpose for the writing, and where it will be published – it's up to you whether you write this onto the plan.
9 Finally, plan your hook – how will you hook the children into the writing? When will you put in the hook?

See Appendix for Circles planning: quick guide.

Skeleton circles plan

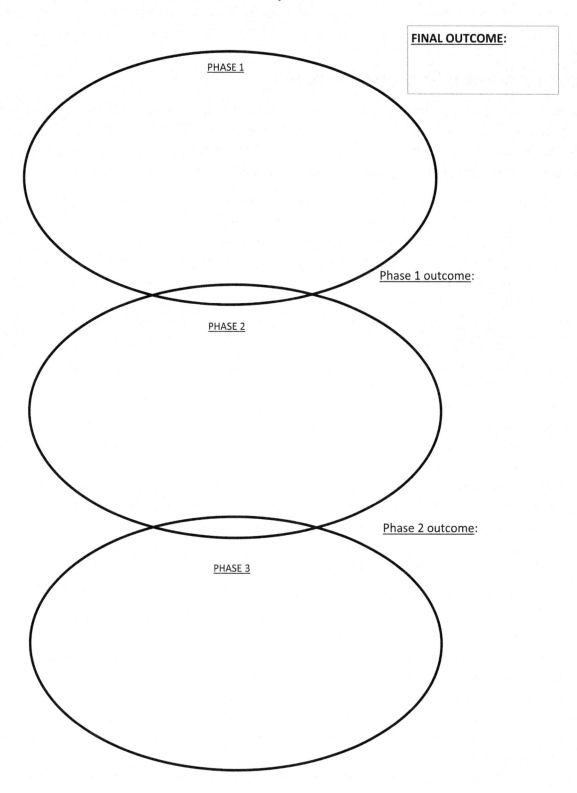

Unit plans

Introduction

This part is divided into two chapters. Each chapter is based on a different hook into writing: picture books, and short stories and novels.

Within each section, divided into Key Stage 1 and Key Stage 2, there are:

1 mind maps showing the different text types that could be stimulated by each hook
2 circles plans that demonstrate how to reach the written outcomes and also that show how the 'hooks' can be used at different points during the teaching sequence

The mind maps are to give you an idea of the breadth and scope of writing that can be stimulated by each 'hook'. Each map has suggestions for four of the following text types: narrative, description, instruction, recount, explanation, information, persuasion, and discussion.

Each circles plan has a suggested key stage. Please note that these are only suggestions based on the age-appropriateness of the hook; teachers may, of course, adapt and amend them to tailor them to their pupils.

Please find below explanations for some terms that are used in the circles plans:

Term	Explanation
Reader response – likes, dislikes, puzzles, patterns (usually Phase 1)	Articulating responses to text helps children to decide what makes it effective. This is an activity that asks children what they liked and disliked; any questions about it; and any patterns that they can see within the text or across other similar texts. *Please note that there is a variety of reader response activities available; this is an example only.*
Compare and contrast (Phase 1)	This is where the teacher guides the pupils through a comparison of texts to identify similarities and differences, and more importantly, which is more effective and why.

Term	Explanation
Mapping/story map/ story board (Phases 1 and 2)	A visual representation of text – usually small pictures – that are in chronological order.
Story mountain (Phases 1 and 2)	A visual representation of the parts of a story that build up to the 'problem' from the opening, and then back down to the ending.
Writer's hints (Phase 1)	Writer's hints (sometimes known as success criteria or checklists) are the identified aspects of text that the pupils may want to use when they write their own – the elements that they have agreed are effective. They are usually collected during phase 1 and should be displayed on a working wall. There should only be three or four hints for younger children, and five or six for older.
Chunk the text or chunks (Phases 1 and 2)	Separate the text into story or text parts so that children can see the underlying plot or text structure. The parts of a story are usually opening, build up, problem, resolution, and ending. Non-fiction text parts vary. Planning for each chunk of text is suggested at phase 2.
Talk/word/language games (Phases 1 and 2)	These provide an opportunity to 'talk the text' before writing. They usually occur when children are gaining an understanding of the language used in certain text types, and are suggested as a fun way to keep children tuned-in to the appropriate words or language.
Orally rehearse (Phase 2)	This is practising sentences (or more) orally in order to say and hear them, and refine them if necessary, before writing.

Short stories and novels section

Due to the nature and length of the texts, the short story mind maps are not as long as those based on novels.

For each novel, it is assumed that the complete novel has been read to the class *before* the unit of work is begun, unless otherwise stated. For novels and short stories, occasionally there are suggestions in the circles plans of places to stop reading in order to allow children to predict what will come next, and in some cases, I have suggested re-reading a few pages – please do read the circles plans thoroughly before sharing the novel or short story with your class.

Using picture books as hooks

Mind maps and unit plans

UNIT PLANS

Recount
Turn the story into a recount told from the point of view of Grace or another character; Grace and Nana's day out; letter from Grace to a relative about the build up to her playing Peter Pan

Persuasion
Grace's speech persuading the class to choose her; speech persuading others to reach their goals; invitation to a performance; advert for a performance; apology letter from Natalie

Amazing Grace by Mary Hoffman

Narrative
Innovate by putting yourself into the story and reach a different goal at school; retell Dick Whittington or a pirate or Anansi story

Information
Famous: girls/women of colour; female authors/illustrators; family trees, my family; my culture/religion

USING PICTURE BOOKS AS HOOKS   17

UNIT PLAN
Theme: *Amazing Grace* – Information Page   Key Stage 1

FINAL OUTCOME
To write a page for a class information book

PHASE 1
- Read a range of information texts
- Explore and respond – which do you prefer and why? Purpose and audience of each?
- Immerse children in information texts about people, cultures and religions
- Identify information page features (including visual elements such as pictures/diagrams)
- Collect and explore transferable vocabulary
- Collect list of writer's hints for information texts

Phase 1 outcome
To know what a good information page looks and sounds like

PHASE 2
- Provide stimulus for new information page (hook); could be a page about you or your culture or religion
- Explore key vocabulary
- Decide on the information that the children will include in their own page
- Plan information page (including 'design' decisions)
- Orally rehearse ideas
- Refine and/or develop them
- Check plan is complete

Phase 2 outcome
To have planned my information page

PHASE 3
- Model how to use plan to write introduction, and shared write
- Independent write of introductions
- Model how to use plan to write next part of information page, and shared write
- Independent write of next parts
- Re-draft elements that need polishing
- Add visuals, e.g. photographs
- Publish, share and evaluate

UNIT PLAN

Theme: *Amazing Grace* – Narrative **Key Stage 1**

FINAL OUTCOME
Write a story on the theme of wanting something

PHASE 1
- Explore and respond to *Amazing Grace* story
- Check children understand the key events and the message in the story
- Use a story map or mountain to chart key events of the story
- Use drama/role-play to understand the key events
- Collect list of writer's hints for the *Amazing Grace* story

Phase 1 outcome
To know what a good story sounds and looks like

PHASE 2
- Discuss times when they really wanted to be chosen to do something
- Use the story map/mountain as a framework for planning a new story
- Use drama/role-play to explore new ideas
- Collect vocabulary along the way
- Replace main events on story map or mountain with new ideas
- Children create a new story map or plan
- Orally rehearse new ideas
- Finalise plan

Phase 2 outcome
To have planned my story

PHASE 3
- Show children mock-up of final book
- Model write opening using story map/plan
- Children write opening independently
- Model write main events using story map/plan
- Children write main events independently
- Model write ending using story map/plan
- Children write ending independently
- Mark, feedback and edit
- Publish and share

USING PICTURE BOOKS AS HOOKS

UNIT PLAN

Theme: *Amazing Grace* – Persuasion   Key Stage 1

FINAL OUTCOME
To write & perform a persuasive speech

PHASE 1

- Play games to tune children into the language of persuasion, e.g. persuade me to give you an extra 20 minutes play
- Re-read the audition part of *Amazing Grace* and explain the task (to think about what Grace might have said to persuade them to vote for her)
- Perform your own short speech as if you were Raj bidding to play Captain Hook
- Shared read your speech and collect effective words and language – check understanding and why they are effective
- Use talk activities to further explore the concept of 'persuasion', including purpose and audience
- Collect writer's hints and add to list of language/vocabulary collected earlier
- Clarify structure of a persuasive speech by chunking your model

Phase 1 outcomes
To know what a good persuasive speech sounds like

PHASE 2

- Use *Amazing Grace* to stimulate ideas about what she might say to persuade her class to vote for her
- Use chunks from phase 1 to start to plan the new persuasive speech
- Use discussion based role-play to explore ideas for elements that would persuade the children to vote for her
- Complete plan

Phase 2 outcome
To have planned my own persuasive speech

PHASE 3

- Shared write first section
- Children independently write first section
- Mark/feedback and children edit/polish
- Shared write next section
- Children independently write next section
- Support with editing and refining
- Practise performing speeches
- Perform and evaluate

UNIT PLANS

Journey by Aaron Becker

Description
Settings; contrasting settings; lantern forest description; flying carpet journey description

Recount
Diary entries; a day in the life of a citizen in 'journey'; recount letter from the purple bird; news recount of the Journey events

Narrative
Write the story of one of the events in the book; write the whole story; write the story of the purple bird; write a sequel; write a new story starting from her drawing the door in her bedroom

Explanation
How the flying machines or balloons work; how to fly a magic carpet; why the purple bird was captured; how to free a purple bird

UNIT PLAN

Theme: *Journey* – Explanation

Key Stage 1

FINAL OUTCOME
Write an explanation of how to fly a magic carpet

PHASE 1

- Play talk games to establish what an explanation is, e.g. explain how you got to school this morning, explain why what makes day and night
- Shared read simple explanation texts
- Explore and respond – likes, dislikes, puzzles, patterns; and identify audience and purpose of each
- Immerse children in explanation texts so that they know the typical language patterns
- Collect effective vocabulary/language of explanations
- Chunk a simple explanation text into parts so that children understand the structure (introduction, chronological explanation of how/why, conclusion)
- Create a list of writer's hints

Phase 1 outcome
To know what a good explanation looks and sounds like

PHASE 2

- Re-visit pages of *Journey* when she is flying on the magic carpet
- Explore ideas around how to fly a magic carpet
- Introduce new technical vocabulary and play talk games for children to orally rehearse
- Use text chunked in phase 1 to help plan new explanation
- Play word/language games to orally rehearse ideas around how to fly a magic carpet and the language of explanation
- Finalise plan

Phase 2 outcome
To have planned my explanation

PHASE 3

- Show children a mock-up of final explanation i.e. how it could be laid out on the page
- Shared write opening of explanation – model how to use plan
- Children independently write the opening
- Mark and follow-up on issues before they move onto the main body of the explanation
- Shared write to support with main body and closing
- Children independently write rest of explanation
- Support them to edit and refine whole text
- Publish, share and evaluate

UNIT PLAN

Theme: *Journey* – Narrative　　　　　　　　　　　　　　　　　　　　　Key Stage 1

FINAL OUTCOME
Write the *Journey* story (simplified)

PHASE 1
- Read *Journey* & respond (likes, dislikes, puzzles, patterns)
- Use a story map or mountain to chunk *Journey* into key events
- Use drama, role-play and discussion to check children's understanding of each event
- Take one event and discuss the language that might be used to 'tell' that part of the story
- Write a model of another event from *Journey*, read and discuss it
- From this model, collect effective vocabulary and language and create list of writer's hints

Phase 1 outcome
To know and understand the *Journey* story

PHASE 2
- Explain task
- Using the story map or mountain as a guide, discuss the main events that will be included in your story (e.g. opening, 3 main events, ending)
- Generate plan
- Use drama/role-play to explore 3 main events, orally rehearse, add ideas to plan
- Collect vocabulary along the way
- Finalise plan

Phase 2 outcome
To have planned my *Journey* story

PHASE 3
- Model write opening using plan
- Children write opening independently
- Model write main events using plan
- Children write main events independently
- Model write ending using plan
- Children write ending independently
- Mark, feedback and edit
- Publish, share and evaluate

USING PICTURE BOOKS AS HOOKS

UNIT PLAN	
Theme: *Journey* – Recount	Key Stage 1

FINAL OUTCOME
Purple Bird's recount

PHASE 1

- Write a model recount based on a known story, e.g. recount letter to the 3 Little Pigs' mother, shared read it and ask for the children's responses
- Discuss purpose and audience for recounts
- Play with the sentence structures and vocabulary in the model so that children are clear about this text-type
- Chunk the model into key events – build a bank of vocabulary for each, and develop children's understanding of this vocabulary
- Use the model to support knowledge of structure and explore the use of time connectives
- Collect writer's hints for a recount

Phase 1 outcome
To know what a good recount looks and sounds like

PHASE 2

- Read *Journey* and chunk the events from the point of view of the purple bird
- Consider where the bird came from and where it was going
- Tell the children that the boy in '*journey*' wants to know where purple bird went – the task is to write a recount for the boy
- Discuss each event; what would the bird say about each?
- Build a new plan of the purple bird's recount, adding detail that takes the audience into account
- Orally rehearse, collecting and enhancing vocabulary
- Finalise plan

Phase 2 outcome
To have planned my recount

PHASE 3

- Shared write opening
- Children write opening independently
- Shared write middle sections
- Children write middle sections independently
- Edit and re-draft as necessary
- Shared write endings
- Children write endings independently
- Mark, feedback and polish drafts
- Publish, share and evaluate

24 UNIT PLANS

Naughty Bus by Jan and Jerry Oke

Captions & Labels
Label a map with places the bus visits; parts of the bus; new captions for the illustrations; create new scenes for the bus and add captions

Instructions
How to: be a naughty bus, clean a naughty bus, rescue a naughty bus from a pond, be a good bus, keep safe on a naughty bus

Narrative
Write Naughty Bus as a short story; change the setting, write a new adventure; choose a different vehicle – Naughty Train, Truck etc; sequel, Naughty Night Bus

Persuasion
Apology email from the bus; email persuading the bus to stop being naughty; persuade the bus to do other naughty things; advert for bus toy; wanted poster

USING PICTURE BOOKS AS HOOKS

UNIT PLAN

Theme: *Naughty Bus* – Instructions   Key Stage 1

FINAL OUTCOME
Write a set of instructions – how to clean a *naughty bus*

PHASE 1

- Explain task – to write a set of instructions for how to clean a *Naughty Bus*
- Shared read various sets of instructions
- Explore and respond – compare & contrast
- Identify the features and typical language of instructions (e.g. introduction, what you need, what you do, imperative verbs, ordered steps, concluding statement)
- Build list of writer's hints for instructions
- Play language games to develop understanding of imperative verb meanings, e.g. mime the action
- Check children understand the chunks of instructions (introduction, what you need, what you do, conclusion)

Phase 1 outcome
To know what a good set of Instructions looks and sounds like

PHASE 2

- Play games that involve the children giving instructions to each other
- Draw out the language and continue to build banks and understanding
- Re-read the cleaning parts of *Naughty Bus* and use drama/role-play to explore the instructions you might give for cleaning a *Naughty Bus*
- Use chunked set of instructions as basis for plan of new set
- Practise use of imperative verbs appropriate to this set of instructions
- Talk activities to support with ideas for what you might put into an introduction, and the 'what you need' section
- Talk activities to support with ideas for adding detail into each step, e.g. look out for old baked beans and bits of pond weed
- Support with ideas for a concluding statement
- Complete plan

Phase 2 outcome
To have planned my instructions

PHASE 3

- Shared write introduction
- Children write introduction and 'what you need' independently
- Shared write initial steps
- Children write steps independently
- Shared write concluding statement
- Children complete independently
- Mark, feedback and edit
- Publish and share

UNIT PLAN

Theme: *Naughty Bus* – Narrative

Key Stage 1

FINAL OUTCOME
Write *Naughty Bus* as a short story

PHASE 1

- Re-read *Naughty Bus* and gather children's responses
- Explain task
- Use a story map or mountain to chunk *Naughty Bus* into key events
- For each key event discuss how the bus is feeling, and how other characters may be feeling
- Shared read popular short stories with similar themes
- Collect writer's hints for what makes a good story

Phase 1 outcome
To know and understand the story of the *Naughty Bus*

PHASE 2

- Using the story map or mountain as a guide, discuss the main events that will be included in your story (e.g. opening, 3 main events, ending)
- Generate plan
- Discuss and bank ideas for how the *Naughty Bus* story would begin, e.g. Many years ago, a boy received a little, red bus for his birthday...
- Take each event and discuss the language that might be used to 'tell' that part of the story
- Discuss and bank ideas for how the *Naughty Bus* story would end, e.g. once the boy had fallen fast asleep a Night Bus adventure began.
- Finalise plan

Phase 2 outcome
To have planned my *Naughty Bus* story

PHASE 3

- Model write opening using plan
- Children write opening independently
- Model write main events using plan
- Children write main events independently
- Mark, feedback and follow up on issues throughout the process
- Model write ending using plan
- Children write ending independently
- Mark, feedback and edit
- Publish, share and evaluate

UNIT PLAN

Theme: *Naughty Bus* – Persuasion
Key Stage 1

FINAL OUTCOME
Apology email from *Naughty Bus*

PHASE 1

- Read *Naughty Bus*, then read email from the bus company telling *Naughty Bus* that he's not allowed to carry passengers anymore because he's too naughty
- Explain task – to write an email from *Naughty Bus* apologising and asking to be reinstated
- General discussion what is persuasion? Explore the different purposes and audiences for persuasion
- Shared read the email from the bus company
- Identify use of language, collect effective language and vocabulary
- Chunk the email into sections
- Build list of writer's hints for persuasive emails

Phase 1 outcome
I know what a good persuasive email looks and sounds like

PHASE 2

- Use drama/role-play to explore what the *Naughty Bus* might say in his email; collect ideas
- Group ideas into themes and generate persuasive sentences – orally rehearse to check that they sound right and have the right effect
- Check children are clear about purpose & audience for email
- Use chunks from phase 1 to plan new email
- Take elements from the list of hints and practise using them
- Orally rehearse each section of the email
- Add vocabulary to plan
- Finalise plan

Phase 2 outcome
I have planned my persuasive email

PHASE 3

- Shared write opening of email – model how to use plan
- Children independently write the opening
- Mark and follow-up on issues before they move onto the main body of the email
- Shared write to support with main body and closing
- Children independently write rest of email
- Support them to edit and refine whole text
- Publish, share and evaluate
- Send emails to the bus company and see if anyone replies!

UNIT PLANS

One Snowy Night by Nick Butterworth

Instructions
Percy's guide to being a park keeper; how to keep animals safe in the snow; park animals' guide to enjoying snowy weather; making hot cocoa

Recount
Diary entry of one of the animals or Percy; a letter from Percy to one of his friends; snowy Night report for Park News

Narrative
Innovate to One: Thundery or Stormy or Rainy Night; change the animals and where they sleep; write the story of what happens the next night

Information
Wiki page about: parks, jobs a park keeper does; animals that feature in the story; snow/snowy weather; Guide to: your local park; snow games; snow sports

USING PICTURE BOOKS AS HOOKS

UNIT PLAN
Theme: *One Snowy Night* – Information Page　　　　　　　　　　　　　　　　Key Stage 1

FINAL OUTCOME
To write an information page about park keepers

PHASE 1
- Read a range of information texts
- Explore and respond – which do you prefer and why? Purpose and audience of each?
- Immerse children in information texts about the jobs people do
- Identify information page features (including visual elements such as pictures/diagrams)
- Collect and explore transferable vocabulary
- Collect list of writer's hints for information texts

Phase 1 outcome
To know what a good information page looks and sounds like

PHASE 2
- Explain task
- Use sources, including the Percy the Park Keeper series, to explore the jobs that park keepers do
- Collect and build relevant vocabulary
- Decide on the information that the children will include in their own page
- Plan information page (including 'design' decisions)
- Orally rehearse ideas
- Refine and/or develop them
- Finalise plan

Phase 2 outcome
To have planned my information page

PHASE 3
- Model how to use plan to write introduction, and shared write
- Independent write of introductions
- Model how to use plan to write next part of information page, and shared write
- Independent write of next parts
- Re-draft elements that need polishing
- Add visuals, e.g. photographs
- Publish, share and evaluate

UNIT PLAN

Theme: *One Snowy Night* – Narrative Key Stage 1

FINAL OUTCOME
One Stormy Night story

PHASE 1

- Read *One Snowy Night* & respond (likes, dislikes, puzzles, patterns); draw comparisons to other similar stories
- Break the story down to check children's comprehension of the plot
- Use a story map or mountain so that children can see the structure of the story
- Build list of writer's hints
- Explain task

Phase 1 outcome
To know *One Snowy Night* and what makes it a good story

PHASE 2

- Use pictures, film and sound stimuli to explore what a stormy night looks, feels and sounds like
- Collect vocabulary
- Discuss which animals would want shelter during a storm
- Map or plan *One Stormy Night* story
- Use word/language games to orally rehearse new vocabulary and language
- Orally rehearse new story
- Finalise plan

Phase 2 outcome
To have planned my story

PHASE 3

- Model write opening using plan
- Children write opening independently
- Model write main events using plan
- Children write main events independently
- Model write ending using plan
- Children write ending independently
- Mark, feedback and edit
- Publish and share

USING PICTURE BOOKS AS HOOKS 31

UNIT PLAN

Theme: *One Snowy Night* – Recount

Key Stage 1

FINAL OUTCOME
Park newsletter recount of *One Snowy Night*

PHASE 1

- Shared read extracts from newsletters and respond
- Discuss purpose and audience for each
- Identify the language of recount within the extracts and collect key vocabulary/language
- Chunk one of the newsletter recounts into parts so that children understand the structure
- Agree what makes a good newsletter recount and collate a list of writer's hints

Phase 1 outcome
To know what a good newsletter recount looks and sounds like

PHASE 2

- Explain that Percy has been asked to write about the snowy night for the park newsletter
- Re-read *One Snowy Night* and identify the main events that Percy will need to write about
- Plan using the chunks identified in phase 1
- Discuss each event and orally rehearse what you might say about it, collecting and enhancing vocabulary
- Finalise plan

Phase 2 outcome
To have planned my newsletter recount

PHASE 3

- Shared write opening
- Children write opening independently
- Shared write middle sections
- Children write middle sections independently
- Edit and re-draft as necessary
- Shared write endings
- Children write endings independently
- Mark, feedback and polish drafts
- Publish, share and evaluate

32 UNIT PLANS

Stick Man by Julia Donaldson & Axel Scheffler

Persuasion
Find Stick Man poster; letters persuading the characters to return Stick Man or not to use him; Stick Lady Love persuading Stick Man not to go out; Advert for the many uses of Stick Man

Instructions
How to: find Stick Man, play pooh sticks, build a snow man, build a sand castle, help Santa deliver presents; Stick Man's route home

Narrative
Turn an event in the story into a new mini story; add in more events; change the ending; write an adventure for the 3 children

Information
Map of Stick Man's journey; Wiki page about Stick Man; games you can play with a stick/stick activities; Stick Man's guide to keeping safe

UNIT PLAN

Theme: *Stick Man* – Information
Key Stage 1

FINAL OUTCOME
To write Wiki page about *Stick Man*

PHASE 1

- Read a range of internet information pages
- Explore and respond – which do you prefer and why? Purpose and audience of each?
- Identify information page features
- Immerse children in information pages about people
- Identify the typical structure of a wiki page about a famous person (e.g. why they are famous, their background, what they're doing now)
- Collect and explore transferable vocabulary
- Collect list of writer's hints for information pages

Phase 1 outcome
To know what a good Wiki page looks and sounds like

PHASE 2

- Explain task
- Support children to decide on the information that they will include in their own page
- Plan Wiki page
- Collect and build relevant vocabulary
- Orally rehearse ideas
- Refine and/or develop them
- Finalise plan

Phase 2 outcome
To have planned my Wiki page

PHASE 3

- Model how to use plan to write introduction, and shared write
- Independent write of introductions
- Model how to use plan to write next part of information page, and shared write
- Independent write of next parts
- Re-draft elements that need polishing
- Add visuals, e.g. photographs
- Publish, share and evaluate

UNIT PLAN		
Theme: *Stick Man* – Instructions		Key Stage 1

FINAL OUTCOME
Write directions for finding *Stick Man*

PHASE 1

- Hide *Stick Man* in the school grounds and write a set of directions for the children to follow to find him
- Explain the task – they are going to hide *Stick Man* and write a set of directions so that you can find him
- Shared read a range of instructions/directions
- Explore and respond – compare & contrast
- Identify the features and typical language of directions
- Build list of writer's hints for directions
- Play language games to develop understanding of the language of directions
- Check children understand the structure of directions (introduction, the directions, conclusion)

Phase 1 outcome
To know what a good set of directions looks and sounds like

PHASE 2

- Play games that involve the children giving directions to each other to follow (can do this in the classroom or school hall)
- Draw out the language and continue to build banks and understanding
- Re-read your original directions to explore the directions the children might give for finding *Stick Man*
- Plan new directions
- Talk activities to support with ideas for what you might put into an introduction
- Talk activities to support with ideas for adding detail into each step, e.g. tiptoe past the Head's office
- Support with ideas for a concluding statement
- Complete plan

Phase 2 outcome
To have planned my directions

PHASE 3

- Shared write introduction
- Children write introduction independently
- Shared write first part of directions
- Children write directions independently
- Shared write concluding statement
- Children complete independently
- Mark, feedback and edit
- Publish and share
- Try them out!

USING PICTURE BOOKS AS HOOKS

UNIT PLAN		
Theme: *Stick Man* – Narrative		Key Stage 1

FINAL OUTCOME
Stick Lady Love story

PHASE 1

- Read *Stick Man* & respond (likes, dislikes, puzzles, patterns)
- Break the story down to check children's comprehension of the plot
- Use a story map or mountain so that children can see the structure of the story
- Explain task (simple *Stick Lady* story, e.g. goes out, things happen to her, arrives home safe – does not need to rhyme, could include a *Stick Lady* refrain)

Phase 1 outcome
To know the *Stick Man* story

PHASE 2

- Explore and collect other uses for a stick, e.g. magic wand, ribbon twirl, conductor's baton, relay baton
- Explore and collect children's ideas for what might happen in the *Stick Lady* story
- Map or plan *Stick Lady* Love story
- Use word/language games to orally rehearse new vocabulary and language
- Clarify ideas for how *Stick Lady* story will end
- Orally rehearse new story
- Finalise plan

Phase 2 outcome
To have planned my story

PHASE 3

- Model write opening using plan
- Children write opening independently
- Model write main events using plan
- Children write main events independently
- Model write ending using plan
- Children write ending independently
- Mark, feedback and edit
- Publish and share

36 UNIT PLANS

Tad by Benji Davies

Description
Settings; characters; pond life; floating/sinking – water movement descriptions; crouching/jumping – frog movement descriptions

Explanation
How to overcome fears; life-cycles; pond life (living processes); how to investigate ponds, e.g. pond dipping, keeping safe

Narrative
Innovate the story, e.g. change the predator or change Tad; a new adventure for Tad; write the fish's story

Information
Tadpoles; frogs; pond life; predators/prey; growing and changing; water safety posters

USING PICTURE BOOKS AS HOOKS   37

UNIT PLAN

Theme: *Tad* – Description   Key Stage 1

FINAL OUTCOME
Write setting descriptions

PHASE 1

- Watch short films of pond life focussing on the underwater setting
- Collect vocabulary and build and bank descriptive language
- Look carefully at some of the illustrations in *Tad* and other related picture books – add to the bank of vocabulary and descriptive language
- Write a short model setting description related to the underwater theme
- Shared read and identify the structure (e.g. big picture view, describe bottom of pond, next 'layer', next 'layer', beneath the surface)
- Collect writer's hints for a setting description

Phase 1 outcome
To know what a good setting description sounds like

PHASE 2

- Choose an underwater illustration that provides the best stimulus for writing a setting description (real life are easier to write than fantasy)
- Identify the most precise vocabulary and description from those already banked
- Pair work – children 'talk' their descriptions
- Plan a description using the structure discussed in phase 1

Phase 2 outcome
To have planned a setting description

PHASE 3

- Model write the first couple of lines of the setting description (including modelling how to work from a plan)
- Children independently write their descriptions
- Mark/feedback, edit and refine
- Provide several picture stimuli for children to choose from for their second setting description
- Children independently plan and write the second description (putting into practice what they have learned from the first)
- Edit, refine and publish

UNIT PLAN

Theme: *Tad* – Explanation
Key Stage 1

FINAL OUTCOME
Life cycle of a frog explanation

PHASE 1

- Play talk games to establish what an explanation is, e.g. explain how you got to school this morning, explain what makes day and night
- Shared read simple science/process related explanation texts
- Explore, respond and identify audience and purpose of each
- Immerse children in explanation texts and bank the typical language patterns
- Collect effective vocabulary/language of explanations
- Chunk a simple explanation text into parts so that children understand the structure (introduction, chronological explanation of process, conclusion)
- Identify layout features (headings, diagrams, pictures) and purpose of each
- Create a list of writer's hints

Phase 1 outcome
To know what a good explanation looks and sounds like

PHASE 2

- Re-cap the lifecycle of a frog
- Introduce new technical vocabulary and play talk games for children to orally rehearse
- Use text chunked in phase 1 to help plan new explanation
- Generate ideas for what might be included in the introduction
- Use pictures to orally rehearse the steps within the frog's lifecycle
- Generate ideas for what might be included in the conclusion
- Finalise plan

Phase 2 outcome
To have planned my explanation

PHASE 3

- Shared write introduction – model how to use plan
- Children independently write the introduction
- Mark and follow-up on issues before they move onto the main body of the explanation
- Shared write to support with main body and conclusion
- Children independently write rest of explanation
- Support them to edit and refine whole text
- Add diagrams, pictures as needed
- Publish, share and evaluate

UNIT PLAN	
Theme: *Tad* – Narrative	Key Stage 1

FINAL OUTCOME
New *Tad* story

PHASE 1

- Read *Tad* & respond (likes, dislikes, puzzles, patterns)
- Break the *Tad* story down to check children's comprehension of the plot
- Use a story mountain so that children can see the main ideas in the story (*Tad* is small, everyone else grows, scared of Big Blub, grows big enough to join the others)
- Shared read other related stories (water themed/fish/frogs)
- Explain task

Phase 1 outcome
To know the *Tad* story and other similar stories

PHASE 2

- Using other stories as a stimulus collect ideas for what *Tad* might be scared of this time (e.g. pond weed, dragon fly, heron)
- Plan using a story mountain
- Collect vocabulary
- Use word/language games to orally rehearse new vocabulary and language
- Orally rehearse new story
- Finalise plan

Phase 2 outcome
To have planned my story

PHASE 3

- Show children mock-up of final book
- Model write opening using plan
- Children write opening independently
- Model write main events using plan
- Children write main events independently
- Model write ending using plan
- Children write ending independently
- Mark, feedback, and edit
- Publish books and share

The Day the Crayons Quit by Drew Daywalt And Oliver Jeffers

Explanation
Why crayons want to quit; how to stop crayons from quitting; why crayons shouldn't quit; how colour mixing works; how crayons are made

Persuasion
Letters from Duncan to persuade the crayons to come back; job advert/wanted posters for new crayons; letters from other important stationery or furniture that wants to quit

Narrative
Turn the book into a story; write an alternative story, e.g. the day the chairs quit; write the story from one of the crayon's or from Duncan's viewpoint

Recount
Letters about their new lives from crayons to Duncan; Duncan's diary about the day the crayons quit; news recount about the events for Duncan's school newsletter

USING PICTURE BOOKS AS HOOKS

UNIT PLAN
Theme: *The Day the Crayons Quit* – Narrative   Key Stage 1

FINAL OUTCOME
Write the story of *the day the crayons quit* (opening provided)

PHASE 1
- Re-read *The Day the Crayons Quit*
- Use a story map or mountain to chunk it into key events
- Discuss who the main characters are and where the story is set
- Focus on the opening and discuss the language that might be used to 'tell' that part of the story
- Write a model of the opening of the story, shared read and discuss it

Phase 1 outcome
To know and understand the story of *the day the crayons quit*

PHASE 2
- Explain task
- Using the story map or mountain as a guide, discuss the main events that will be included in your story (e.g. opening, main crayons that quit and their reasons, ending)
- Take each part in turn and discuss the language that might be used to 'tell' that part of the story
- Generate plan (opening is already done)

Phase 2 outcome
To have planned my story

PHASE 3
- Shared read opening
- Give children opening to stick into books
- Model write main events using plan
- Children write main events independently
- Model write ending using plan
- Children write ending independently
- Mark, feedback and edit
- Publish, share and evaluate

UNIT PLAN

Theme: *The Day the Crayons Quit* – Persuasion

Key Stage 1

FINAL OUTCOME
Persuasive letter to a crayon

PHASE 1

- Choose two letters from the crayons to read aloud
- Discuss the main arguments that each crayon is making
- Discuss what Duncan might say in response to each of them
- General discussion on what persuasion is and when we use it
- Write a model response letter to beige crayon
- Shared read and respond
- Identify use of language, collect effective language and vocabulary
- Chunk the letter into sections
- Build list of writer's hints for persuasive letters

Phase 1 outcome
I know what a good persuasive letter looks and sounds like

PHASE 2

- Re-read the other crayons' letters and ask the children to choose the letter that they want to reply to
- Group the children according to what they choose; groups discuss how they might respond
- Use chunks from phase 1 to plan new letters
- Take elements from the list of hints and practise using them
- Orally rehearse each section of the letter
- Add vocabulary to plan
- Finalise plan

Phase 2 outcome
I have planned my persuasive letter

PHASE 3

- Shared write opening of reply letter – model how to use plan
- Children independently write the opening
- Mark and follow-up on issues before they move onto the main body of the letter
- Shared write to support with main body and closing
- Children independently write rest of letter
- Support them to edit and refine whole text
- Publish, share and evaluate
- Send letters to the crayons and see if anyone replies!

UNIT PLAN	
Theme: *The Day the Crayons Quit* – Recount	Key Stage 1

FINAL OUTCOME
School newsletter – crayons quit recount

PHASE 1

- Shared read extracts from school newsletters and respond
- Discuss purpose and audience for each
- Identify the language of recount within the extracts and collect key vocabulary/language
- Chunk one of the newsletter recounts into parts so that children understand the structure
- Agree what makes a good school newsletter recount and collate a list of writer's hints

Phase 1 outcome
To know what a good newsletter recount looks and sounds like

PHASE 2

- Explain that Duncan has been asked to write about the crayons quitting for the school newsletter
- Re-read *The Day the Crayons Quit* and identify the main events that Duncan will need to write about
- Plan using the chunks identified in phase 1
- Discuss each event and orally rehearse what you might say about it, collecting and enhancing vocabulary
- Finalise plan

Phase 2 outcome
To have planned my newsletter recount

PHASE 3

- Shared write opening
- Children write opening independently
- Shared write middle sections
- Children write middle sections independently
- Edit and re-draft as necessary
- Shared write endings
- Children write endings independently
- Mark, feedback and polish drafts
- Publish, share and evaluate

44 UNIT PLANS

The Disgusting Sandwich by Gareth Edwards & Hannah Shaw

Description
Use adjectives and expanded noun phrases and create new descriptive sentences; find synonyms and develop sentences; use verbs and synonyms to develop 'action' sentences

Instructions
Sandwich making; disgusting sandwich recipes; feeding animals/pets; recipes for picnics

Narrative
Innovate the story by changing the sandwich, characters and/or setting; retell the story from the sandwich or badger's point of view

Recount
The disgusting sandwich's day from the point of view of the sandwich or the badger; a day at the park

USING PICTURE BOOKS AS HOOKS 45

UNIT PLAN
Theme: *The Disgusting Sandwich* – Instructions   Key Stage 1

FINAL OUTCOME
Write a set of instructions for a disgusting sandwich

PHASE 1

- Explain task – to write a set of instructions for how to make a disgusting sandwich (*decide whether to follow what happens in the book or write a nasty recipe)
- Shared read various sets of instructions/recipes
- Explore and respond – compare & contrast
- Identify the features and typical language of instructions (e.g. introduction, what you need, what you do, imperative verbs, ordered steps, concluding statement)
- Build list of writer's hints for instructions/recipes
- Play language games to develop understanding of imperative verb meanings, e.g. mime the action
- Check children understand the chunks of instructions

Phase 1 outcome
To know what a good set of Instructions looks and sounds like

PHASE 2

- Play games that involve the children giving instructions to each other
- Draw out the language and continue to build banks and understanding
- Re-read *The Disgusting Sandwich* and use drama/role-play to explore the instructions you might give for creating a disgusting sandwich (*or discuss what might be in a disgusting sandwich recipe)
- Use chunked set of instructions as basis for plan of new set
- Practise use of imperative verbs appropriate to this set of instructions
- Talk activities to support with ideas for what you might put into an introduction, and the 'what you need' section
- Talk activities to support with ideas for adding detail into each step, e.g. Make sure you ride across the sandwich on a skateboard
- Support with ideas for a concluding statement
- Complete plan

Phase 2 outcome
To have planned my instructions

PHASE 3

- Shared write introduction
- Children write introduction and 'what you need' independently
- Shared write initial steps
- Children write steps independently
- Shared write concluding statement
- Children complete independently
- Mark, feedback and edit
- Publish and share

UNIT PLAN

Theme: *The Disgusting Sandwich* – Narrative

Key Stage 1

FINAL OUTCOME
Write The Disgusting _____ story

PHASE 1

- Read *The Disgusting Sandwich* & respond (likes, dislikes, puzzles, patterns)
- Break the story down to check children's comprehension of the plot
- Chunk it into sections so that children can see the structure of the story
- Collect effective vocabulary and language – check understanding of effect
- Build list of writer's hints

Phase 1 outcome
To know *The Disgusting Sandwich* story and what makes it a good story

PHASE 2

- Discuss other food items that the boy might take to the park
- Use drama/role-play to explore what might have happened to it this time
- Collect vocabulary along the way
- Map or plan new Disgusting _____ story
- Use word/language games to orally re-hearse new vocabulary and language
- Orally rehearse new story
- Finalise plan

Phase 2 outcome
To have planned my story

PHASE 3

- Model write opening using plan
- Children write opening independently
- Model write main events using plan
- Children write main events independently
- Model write ending using plan
- Children write ending independently
- Mark, feedback and edit
- Publish and share

USING PICTURE BOOKS AS HOOKS

UNIT PLAN
Theme: *The Disgusting Sandwich* – Recount   Key Stage 1

FINAL OUTCOME
To write the badger's day at the park

PHASE 1

- Write a model recount about a day at a park, shared read it and ask for the children's responses
- Discuss purpose and audience for recounts
- Play with the sentence structures and vocabulary in the model so that children are clear about this text-type
- Chunk the model into key events – build a bank of vocabulary for each, and develop children's understanding of this vocabulary
- Use the model to support knowledge of structure and explore the use of time connectives
- Collect writer's hints for a recount

Phase 1 outcome
To know what a good recount looks and sounds like

PHASE 2

- Read *The Disgusting Sandwich* and chunk the events from the point of view of the badger
- Ask the children who the badger might tell about his day? (This will be the imaginary audience for their writing)
- Discuss each event; what would the badger say about each?
- Build a new plan of the badger's recount, adding detail that takes the audience into account
- Orally rehearse, collecting and enhancing vocabulary
- Finalise plan

Phase 2 outcome
To have planned my recount

PHASE 3

- Shared write opening
- Children write opening independently
- Shared write middle sections
- Children write middle sections independently
- Edit and re-draft as necessary
- Shared write endings
- Children write endings independently
- Mark, feedback and polish drafts
- Publish, share and evaluate

The Lighthouse Keeper's Lunch by Ronda & David Armitage

Description
Settings: sea, lighthouse, cliffs/scenery; Characters: Mr and Mrs Grinling; Hamish the cat; Seagulls and other sea birds; food; boats; travelling on a boat; zipwire

Instructions
Mrs Grinling's recipes; seagulls' guide to how to steal food; Light House Keeper's guide to keeping seagulls away from food

Narrative
Write the Boat Keeper's Lunch story; write the story from a seagull's or the cat's point of view; innovate the foods in the story

Explanation
How lighthouses work; what lighthouses are for; how the Grinlings scared the seagulls; why pet cats don't like water

USING PICTURE BOOKS AS HOOKS 49

UNIT PLAN	
Theme: *The Lighthouse Keeper's Lunch* – Description	Key Stage 1

FINAL OUTCOME
Write character descriptions

PHASE 1

- Shared read a variety of character descriptions (preferably known characters such as Mr & Mrs Twit, Big Bad Wolf, Paddington etc.)
- Compare and contrast – which are effective and why?
- Collect writer's hints
- Collect descriptive language and vocabulary
- Identify the structure of a typical character description
- Re-read *The Lighthouse Keeper's Lunch*, focussing on Mr and Mrs Grinling's characters

Phase 1 outcome
To know what a good character description sounds like

PHASE 2

- Use picture stimulus to generate ideas and vocabulary about the two different characters
- Play word/language games to develop the language of description
- Use role-play to support the children with ideas for the character descriptions – physical description and characteristics, and create two short plans
- Pair work – children 'talk' their descriptions
- Finalise plans

Phase 2 outcome
To have planned my character descriptions

PHASE 3

- For the first Grinling character: Model write first couple of lines (including modelling how to work from a plan)
- Children independently write their descriptions
- Mark/feedback, edit and refine
- Children independently write the second Grinling character description (putting into practice what they have learned from the first)
- Edit, refine and publish

UNIT PLAN

Theme: *The Lighthouse Keeper's Lunch* – Explanation

Key Stage 1

FINAL OUTCOME
Write an explanation of how the Grinlings scared off the seagulls

PHASE 1
- Play talk games to establish what an explanation is, e.g. explain how you got to school this morning, explain what makes day and night
- Shared read simple explanation texts
- Explore and respond – likes, dislikes, puzzles, patterns; and identify audience and purpose of each
- Immerse children in explanation texts so that they know the typical language patterns
- Collect effective vocabulary/language of explanations
- Chunk a simple explanation text into parts so that children understand the structure (introduction, chronological explanation of how/why, conclusion)
- Create a list of writer's hints

Phase 1 outcome
To know what a good explanation looks and sounds like

PHASE 2
- Re-read *The Lighthouse Keeper's Lunch* and identify the steps the Grinlings took to scare off the seagulls
- Introduce new technical vocabulary and play talk games for children to orally rehearse
- Use text chunked in phase 1 to help plan new explanation
- Play word/language games to orally rehearse ideas around how the Grinlings scared off the seagulls explanation
- Finalise plan

Phase 2 outcome
To have planned my explanation

PHASE 3
- Shared write opening of explanation – model how to use plan
- Children independently write the opening
- Mark and follow-up on issues before they move onto the main body of the explanation
- Shared write to support with main body and closing
- Children independently write rest of explanation
- Support them to edit and refine whole text
- Publish, share and evaluate

USING PICTURE BOOKS AS HOOKS 51

UNIT PLAN
Theme: *The Lighthouse Keeper's Lunch* – Narrative   Key Stage 1

FINAL OUTCOME
The Lighthouse Keeper's Lunch story with new food

PHASE 1

- Read *The Lighthouse Keeper's Lunch* & respond (likes, dislikes, puzzles, patterns)
- Break the story down to check children's comprehension of the plot
- Chunk it into sections so that children can see the structure of the story
- Collect effective vocabulary and language – check understanding of effect

Phase 1 outcome
To know *The Lighthouse Keeper's Lunch* story and what makes it a good story

PHASE 2

- Discuss other food items that Mr Grinling might like and that Mrs Grinling could have used to trick the seagulls
- Collect useful vocabulary
- Map or plan new story using different foods
- Use word/language games to orally rehearse new vocabulary and language
- Orally rehearse new story
- Finalise plan

Phase 2 outcome
To have planned my story

PHASE 3

- Model write opening using plan
- Children write opening independently
- Model write main events using plan
- Children write main events independently
- Model write ending using plan
- Children write ending independently
- Mark, feedback and edit
- Publish and share

The Tear Thief by Carol Ann Duffy & Nicoletta Ceccoli

Description
Focus on different aspects of powerful narrative: verbs, adjectives, expanded noun phrases, personification; collect and practise using in new sentences and in short writes; character description

Instructions
How to be a tear thief; how to turn tears into the moon; the tear thief's route map; warning notices/signs about the tear thief

Narrative
Different type of thief story, e.g. the frown thief, the sulk thief; further adventures of the tear thief; tell the story from the sack's point of view

Recount
Diary of the tear thief; postcard from the tear thief; letter from the girl who lost her dog; news recount

UNIT PLAN

Theme: *The Tear Thief* – Description

Key Stage 1

FINAL OUTCOME
Write character descriptions

PHASE 1

- Shared read a variety of character descriptions
- Respond, compare and contrast — which are effective and why?
- Collect writer's hints
- Collect descriptive language
- Identify the structure of a typical character description
- Read the parts of *The Tear Thief* which describe the tear thief; discuss illustrations of *the tear thief*

Phase 1 outcome
To know what a good character description sounds like

PHASE 2

- Collect vocabulary and add to the bank created in phase 1
- Play word/language games to develop the language of description
- Using the structure identified at phase 1, generate ideas and begin to plan for writing a description of *the tear thief*
- Pair work – children 'talk' their descriptions
- Finalise plans

Phase 2 outcome
To have planned my character descriptions

PHASE 3

- Model write first couple of lines (including modelling how to work from a plan)
- Children independently write their descriptions
- Mark/feedback, edit and refine
- Children independently plan and write a second character description, e.g. the sulk thief (putting into practice what they have learned from the first)
- Edit, refine, and publish

UNIT PLAN

Theme: *The Tear Thief* – **Instructions**

Key Stage 1

FINAL OUTCOME
Write a set of instructions for how to be a tear thief

PHASE 1

- Explain task – to write a set of instructions for how to be a tear thief
- Shared read various sets of instructions (include those relevant to this task, e.g. how to keep your teeth clean, how to look after a pet), discuss audience for each
- Explore and respond – compare & contrast
- Identify the features and typical language of instructions, e.g. imperative verbs, ordered steps with some details
- Build list of writer's hints for instructions
- Play language games to develop understanding of imperative verb meanings, e.g. mime the action
- Check children understand the chunks of instructions (introduction, what you need, what you do, conclusion)

Phase 1 outcome
To know what a good set of Instructions looks and sounds like

PHASE 2

- Explain the task; discuss who the audience might be
- Re-read *The Tear Thief* and collect ideas for what you need to do to be a tear thief
- Use drama/role-play to explore the instructions you might give for being a tear thief
- Use chunked set of instructions as basis for plan
- Practise use of imperative verbs appropriate to this set of instructions
- Talk activities to support with ideas for what you might put into an introduction, and the 'what you need' section
- Talk activities to support with ideas for adding detail into each step, e.g. be careful of crocodile tears
- Support with ideas for a concluding statement
- Complete plan

Phase 2 outcome
To have planned my instructions

PHASE 3

- Remind children of the audience for these instructions
- Shared write introduction
- Children write introduction and 'what you need' independently
- Shared write initial steps
- Children write steps independently
- Shared write concluding statement
- Children complete independently
- Mark, feedback and edit
- Publish and share

UNIT PLAN

Theme: *The Tear Thief* – Narrative   Key Stage 1

FINAL OUTCOME
The sulk thief story

PHASE 1

- Re-read *The Tear Thief* & respond (likes, dislikes, puzzles, patterns)
- Break the story down to check children's comprehension of the plot
- Use a story map or mountain so that children can see the structure of the story (can simplify by taking out some events)
- Discuss the characters
- Collect effective language and vocabulary around the tear thief's character and actions
- Build list of writer's hints

Phase 1 outcome
To know *The Tear Thief* and what makes it a good story

PHASE 2

- Explain task
- Use pictures and films to explore what sulking is. Who might sulk? Why?
- Discuss what a sulk thief might look like and how would it/s/he collect sulks?
- Collect and bank vocabulary
- Map or plan *The Sulk Thief* story
- Use word/language games to orally rehearse new vocabulary and language
- Orally rehearse new story
- Finalise plan

Phase 2 outcome
To have planned my story

PHASE 3

- Show children mock-up of book
- Model write opening using plan
- Children write opening independently
- Model write main events using plan
- Children write main events independently
- Model write ending using plan
- Children write ending independently
- Mark, feedback and edit
- Publish and share

UNIT PLANS

The Tiger who Came to Tea by Judith Kerr

Lists
What the tiger ate; what the tiger drank; mummy and Sophie's shopping list; the people who visited that day; café menu; home menu.

Recount
From tiger or mummy or Sophie's viewpoint recount of the day he came to tea; letter to Tiger's keeper about him coming for tea; news recount in style of local newspaper

Narrative
New animal who came to tea story; Sequel, the tiger who came for breakfast; character description of the tiger; new adventure for the tiger – the tiger who...

Persuasion
Invitation for the tiger; letter to persuade parent to invite a tiger for tea; advert to tigers who may want to come to tea

UNIT PLAN
Theme: *The Tiger Who Came to Tea* – **Invitation & Menu**   Key Stage 1

FINAL OUTCOME
Invitation & Menu

PHASE 1
- Re-read *The Tiger Who Came to Tea*
- Explain task – to write an invitation to send to the tiger
- General discussion about invitations – when and why do people send them (purpose & audience)
- Shared read invitations
- Identify use of language, collect effective language and vocabulary
- Build list of writer's hints for invitations

Phase 1 outcome
I know what a good invitation looks and sounds like

PHASE 2
- Generate ideas for what might be on the invitation to the tiger
- Shared write an invitation to the tiger, using the writer's hints
- Children independently write invitations
- Feedback, refine and publish
- Send the invitations and see if the tiger is coming for tea

Phase 2 outcome
I have written an invitation

PHASE 3
- Read a reply from the tiger that accepts your invitation however requests to see a menu (he wants to check that the same food and drink will be available)
- Using the book, compile a list of food and drink that the tiger ate
- Shared read menus
- Model write a menu
- Children independently write a menu to send to the tiger
- Feedback, refine and publish
- Send to the tiger

UNIT PLAN

Theme: *The Tiger Who Came to Tea* – Narrative

Key Stage 1

FINAL OUTCOME
The _____ who came to tea story

PHASE 1

- Read *The Tiger Who Came to Tea* & respond
- Break the story down to check children's comprehension of the plot
- Use a story mountain or map to chunk it into sections so that children can see the structure of the story
- Focussing on the food and drink, collect effective vocabulary and language – check understanding of effect

Phase 1 outcome
To know *The Tiger Who Came to Tea* story and what makes it a good story

PHASE 2

- Explain task
- Discuss other animals/things that could come for tea
- Support the children to choose then discuss what it could eat/drink
- Bank ideas
- Map or plan new story
- Use word/language games to orally rehearse new vocabulary and language
- Orally rehearse new story
- Finalise plan

Phase 2 outcome
To have planned my story

PHASE 3

- Show mock-up of book
- Model write opening using plan
- Children write opening independently
- Model write main events using plan
- Children write main events independently
- Model write ending using plan
- Children write ending independently
- Mark, feedback and edit
- Publish and share

USING PICTURE BOOKS AS HOOKS 59

UNIT PLAN	
Theme: *The Tiger Who Came to Tea* – Recount	Key Stage 1

FINAL OUTCOME
Sophie's diary entry

PHASE 1

- Write a model diary entry from Sophie's mummy's point of view
- Discuss purpose and audience for diaries and explain that they are recounts
- Shared read other diary entries
- Play with the sentence structures and vocabulary in the model so that children are clear about this text-type
- Chunk the model into key events – build a bank of vocabulary for each, and develop children's understanding of this vocabulary
- Use the model to support knowledge of structure and explore the use of time connectives
- Collect writer's hints for a diary entry

Phase 1 outcome
To know what a good diary entry looks and sounds like

PHASE 2

- Read *The Tiger Who Came to Tea* and chunk the events from Sophie's point of view
- Discuss each event; what would Sophie say about each?
- Build a new plan of Sophie's diary
- Orally rehearse, collecting and enhancing vocabulary
- Finalise plan

Phase 2 outcome
To have planned my diary entry

PHASE 3

- Shared write opening
- Children write opening independently
- Shared write middle sections
- Children write middle sections independently
- Edit and re-draft as necessary
- Shared write endings
- Children write endings independently
- Mark, feedback and polish drafts
- Publish, share and evaluate

60 UNIT PLANS

The Way Back Home by Oliver Jeffers

Persuasion
Safety poster; martian wanted poster; help me letter from martian; come to the moon advert; visit Earth advert (for martian)

Recount
About the boy's day; about the martian's day; sequel/walkie-talkie events; recount about new adventure

Narrative
Innovate the story, change where he goes, who he meets and how he gets home; write the martian's story; write another adventure for the boy and martian; sequel using walkie-talkie prompt

Information
Aeroplanes; flying machines; space travel; UFOs; martians; space; light/dark

USING PICTURE BOOKS AS HOOKS 61

UNIT PLAN	
Theme: *The Way Back Home* – Information Page	Key Stage 1

FINAL OUTCOME
To write a page for a class information book

PHASE 1

- Read a range of information texts
- Explore and respond – which do you prefer and why? Purpose and audience of each?
- Immerse children in information texts about light/dark, space, solar system
- Identify information page features (including visual elements such as pictures/diagrams)
- Collect and explore transferable vocabulary
- Collect list of writer's hints for information texts

Phase 1 outcome
To know what a good information page looks and sounds like

PHASE 2

- Explain that the children are going to write a page for a class book on space
- Support them to choose a topic to write about, group children according to chosen topic
- In groups explore key vocabulary
- Decide on the information that the children will include in their own page
- Plan information page (including 'design' decisions)
- In groups orally rehearse ideas
- Check plan is complete

Phase 2 outcome
To have planned my information page

PHASE 3

- Model how to use plan to write introduction, and shared write
- Independent write of introductions
- Model how to use plan to write next part of information page, and shared write
- Independent write of next parts
- Re-draft elements that need polishing
- Add visuals, e.g. photographs
- Publish, share and evaluate

UNIT PLAN

Theme: *The Way Back Home* – Narrative Key Stage 1

FINAL OUTCOME
New Way Back Home story

PHASE 1

- Read *The Way Back Home* & respond (likes, dislikes, puzzles, patterns)
- Make links to, and shared read, other similar stories
- Break *The Way Back Home* down to check children's comprehension of the plot
- Use a story mountain so that children can see the main ideas in the story (boy goes on a journey, gets stuck, meets someone else who's stuck, gets help, both go home)
- Explain task

Phase 1 outcome
To know *The Way Back Home* story

PHASE 2

- Using other stories as a stimulus collect ideas for changes to the: aeroplane, moon, who he meets
- Plan changed story using a story mountain
- Collect ideas for how the new story will end
- Collect vocabulary for each new aspect
- Orally rehearse new story
- Finalise plan

Phase 2 outcome
To have planned my story

PHASE 3

- Show children mock-up of final book
- Model write opening using plan
- Children write opening independently
- Model write main events using plan
- Children write main events independently
- Model write ending using plan
- Children write ending independently
- Mark, feedback and edit
- Publish books and share

USING PICTURE BOOKS AS HOOKS 63

UNIT PLAN	
Theme: *The Way Back Home* – Persuasion	Key Stage 1

FINAL OUTCOME
Attractions on Earth persuasive leaflet

PHASE 1

- Re-read *The Way Back Home*; read a letter that you have received from the boy asking for help with persuading the Martian to visit Earth
- Explain task – to write a persuasive leaflet to send to the Martian
- General discussion what is persuasion? Explore the different purposes and audiences for persuasion.
- Shared read persuasive leaflets
- Identify use of language, collect effective language and vocabulary
- Chunk the leaflet into 5 sections (introduction, 3 attractions on Earth, conclusion)
- Build list of writer's hints for persuasive leaflets

Phase 1 outcome
I know what a good persuasive leaflet looks and sounds like

PHASE 2

- Use picture stimulus to gather ideas around the 3 attractions on Earth; bank ideas
- Group ideas into themes and generate persuasive sentences – orally rehearse to check that they sound right and have the right effect
- Check children are clear about purpose & audience for leaflet
- Use chunks from phase 1 to plan new leaflet
- Generate ideas for what might go into the introduction and conclusion sections
- Orally rehearse each section
- Add vocabulary to plan
- Finalise plan

Phase 2 outcome
I have planned my persuasive leaflet

PHASE 3

- Shared write introduction – model how to use plan
- Children independently write the introduction
- Mark and follow-up on issues before they move onto the main body of the leaflet
- Shared write to support with main body and conclusion
- Children independently write rest of leaflet
- Support them to edit and refine whole text
- Publish, share and evaluate
- Send leaflets to the Martian and see if it replies!

Mind maps and unit plans

UNIT PLANS

Ahmed and the Feather Girl by Jane Ray

Instructions
How to make a feather coat; how to be a feather girl; how to live in a travelling circus; how to fly; Madame Saleem's guide to people management

Recount
Diary entries of: Ahmed, Aurelia, Madame Saleem; News: Girl hatched from golden egg; Feather Girl spotted; Letters from/to Ahmed/Aurelia

Narrative
Prequel (Ahmed's story); sequel; change the feather girl for a different character; setting descriptions; character descriptions

Discussion
Should animals perform for entertainment? Circuses are out of date. Is it ever OK to steal? Children should be allowed to work.

UNIT PLAN
Theme: *Ahmed and the Feather Girl* – Instructions

FINAL OUTCOME
Write instructions for making a feather coat

PHASE 1
- Re-read *Ahmed and the Feather Girl*
- Explain task – to write a set of instructions on making a feather coat for Ahmed to follow
- Shared read various sets of instructions
- Explore and respond – compare & contrast
- Identify the features and typical language of instructions (e.g. introduction, what you need, what you do, imperative verbs, ordered steps, concluding statement)
- Collect writer's hints for instructions
- Play language games to develop understanding of the use of precise vocabulary and of detailed steps within instructions
- Chunk text into sections and discuss layout (refer to purpose and audience)

Phase 1 outcome
To know what a good set of Instructions looks and sounds like

PHASE 2
- Using the 'what you do' section as a starting point for planning begin to orally rehearse and then plan each step
- Use talk activities to support with ideas for adding detail into each step
- Based on what is in the 'what you do' section, discuss what you might put into the 'what you need' section. Add to plan.
- Use talk activities to support with ideas for what you might put into an introduction and a conclusion
- Complete plan
- Discuss other elements that may be included, e.g. pictures and diagrams

Phase 2 outcome
To have planned my instructions

PHASE 3
- Shared write introduction
- Children write introduction and 'what you need' independently
- Shared write initial steps
- Children write steps independently
- Shared write concluding statement
- Children complete independently
- Mark, feedback and edit
- Children put in other aspects such as pictures
- Publish, share and evaluate (perhaps have a go at making a feather coat!)

UNIT PLAN

Theme: *Ahmed and the Feather Girl* – Narrative

Key Stage 2

FINAL OUTCOME
Write a new story – Ahmed and the XX Girl/Boy

PHASE 1

- Read and respond to *Ahmed and the Feather Girl*
- Use drama and role-play to explore the main characters
- Discuss in detail the Feather Girl (Aurelia) – her character and her journey through the story
- Use drama to explore the plot, checking that children understand the key events
- Use a map or story mountain to demonstrate the plot structure
- Explore meanings and bank new vocabulary
- Collect hints – what makes this a good story?

Phase 1 outcome
To know *Ahmed and the Feather Girl* story

PHASE 2

- Explain task
- Building on work on Aurelia's character in phase 1, explore other characters that would work in this story
- Provide opportunities to explore other innovations that could be made to the story, e.g. changing the setting, changing Ahmed's situation
- Generate a plan using the map or mountain created in phase 1 for structure
- Use talk activities to explore how best to use new vocabulary
- Orally rehearse main ideas
- Finalise plan

Phase 2 outcome
To have planned my story

PHASE 3

- Mock-up finished Ahmed and the XXX book so that children can picture their end product
- Brief shared write to get children started
- Children independently write the first paragraph
- Mark and follow-up on issues before they move onto the other parts
- Shared write to support, where necessary
- Children independently write rest of the story
- Support them to edit and refine the story
- Publish, share and evaluate

USING PICTURE BOOKS AS HOOKS

UNIT PLAN	
Theme: *Ahmed and the Feather Girl* – News Report	Key Stage 2

FINAL OUTCOME
To write a news report – Girl Hatches From Golden Egg!

PHASE 1

- Hook – watch short news reels or read news articles about strange events
- General discussion re news of this nature: audience, purpose, tone, form? How it is handled; sensationalism
- Write a model news report about a strange event and immerse the children in it
- Identify use of language and play language games to familiarise the children with it
- Plot the structure and check understanding (headline, 5 Ws intro para, story para, background/ eye-witness para, concluding para)
- Collect writer's hints for a news report

Phase 1 outcome
I know what a good news report sounds like

PHASE 2

- Re-read *Ahmed and the Feather Girl* and stop at The Girl Hatched From A Golden Egg
- Discuss the focus and key events that you could report on in a news report and explore through drama/freeze framing
- Hot seat characters and other parties to collect and develop ideas (including quotes), e.g. Mme Saleem, circus people, visitors
- Support children to plan their reports
- Orally rehearse use of journalistic language; record key ideas
- Check plan against writer's hints, add to plan
- Finalise plan

Phase 2 outcome
To have planned my own news report

PHASE 3

- Shared write opening, incl. headline and use of language
- Independent & guided write openings
- Shared write next parts picking up on issues as report progresses
- Support with concluding paragraph – check it has impact
- Peer evaluate success, then edit
- Publish

UNIT PLANS

Pandora
by
Victoria Turnbull

Description
Settings; contrasting settings; faraway lands; inside Pandora's home; Pandora

Instructions
Junk modelling; upcycling; reducing your waste; looking after an injured bird; planting and growing; keeping safe in the sun; looking after each other; stopping loneliness

Narrative
Write the bird's story; change where Pandora's home is; expand on parts of the story; prequel; sequel

Recount
Pandora's diary; the bird's diary; magazine article about Pandora's life; news recount found in the land of broken things; news recount from the land of living things

USING PICTURE BOOKS AS HOOKS

UNIT PLAN

Theme: *Pandora* – Setting Description   Key Stage 2

FINAL OUTCOME
Write two setting descriptions (inside & outside)

PHASE 1

- Shared read variety of good quality setting descriptions
- Immerse children in setting descriptions so that they know the language structures by heart
- Collect writer's hints
- Play word/language games to develop the language of description (use short film clips & pictures as stimulus)
- Explore the use of expanded noun phrases; metaphors, onomatopoeia, alliteration to add detail and effect
- Collect vocabulary and language
- Chunk a setting description into parts so that children understand structure
- Hook – having read Pandora, collect ideas about the different settings featured

Phase 1 outcome
To know what a good setting description sounds like

PHASE 2

- Explain task – to write two setting descriptions, one of Pandora's house and one about the "land of broken things"
- For each setting begin with generating vocabulary and build a bank for each
- Play word/language games to continue to develop ideas, including use of the senses; expand the banked vocabulary with metaphors, onomatopoeia and alliteration
- Support the children to create a plan for each setting description
- Support children to 'talk' their descriptions to orally rehearse and refine them
- Finalise plans

Phase 2 outcome
To have planned my setting descriptions

PHASE 3

- For one of the settings: Model write first couple of lines (including modelling how to work from a plan)
- Children independently write their descriptions
- Share and refine
- Children independently write the second descriptions (putting into practice what they have learned from first setting descriptions)
- Edit, refine and publish
- Evaluate

UNIT PLAN

Theme: *Pandora* – Instructions

Key Stage 2

FINAL OUTCOME
Write a set of instructions on upcycling

PHASE 1

- Hook – Focus on the page in *Pandora* that ends with "But no one came to visit." Look at the illustration of her home and discuss how she has made furniture out of people's rubbish
- Explain task – to write a set of instructions for upcycling
- Shared read a range of instructions (select sophisticated & varied types of instructions) and discuss audience, tone and form of each
- Re-cap the features and typical language of instructions (e.g. introduction, what you need, what you do, imperative verbs, ordered steps, concluding statement)
- Collect writer's hints for instructions
- Collect and explore new vocabulary

Phase 1 outcome
To know what a good set of Instructions looks and sounds like

PHASE 2

- Shared read information on upcycling
- Provide an opportunity for children to do or observe the upcycling of a piece of furniture, e.g. a wooden chair
- Record, in note form, the process including what they need
- Using the 'what you do' box as a starting point for planning, begin to orally rehearse and then plan each step
- Use talk activities to support with ideas for adding detail into each step, e.g. protect the work area with newspaper or wear a protective mask when sanding
- Plan the 'what you need' part
- Use talk activities to support with ideas for what you might put into an introduction and conclusion
- Finalise plan

Phase 2 outcome
To have planned my instructions

PHASE 3

- Shared write introduction
- Children write introduction and 'what you need' independently
- Shared write 'what you do' section, model how to add detail
- Children write 'what you do' section independently
- Shared write concluding statement
- Children complete independently
- Mark, feedback and edit
- Publish, share and evaluate

USING PICTURE BOOKS AS HOOKS 73

UNIT PLAN	
Theme: *Pandora* – Narrative	Key Stage 2

FINAL OUTCOME
To write a sequel to *Pandora*

PHASE 1

- Re-read *Pandora* and ask the children to consider where Pandora is now and what she is doing
- Consider what her setting looks like now, how is it different?
- Discuss story sequels (e.g. Harry Potter, Alice Through the Looking Glass, Narnia, Charlie & the Great Glass Elevator) – likes/dislikes
- Collect list of writer's hints for what makes a good sequel

Phase 1 outcome
To know what makes a good story sequel

PHASE 2

- Support children to think about a sequel for Pandora, starting with using drama to generate ideas for the main event of the story
- Now generate ideas for the build-up and the resolution
- Support children to create a plan using a storyboard, mountain or planning grid
- Generate ideas for the ending
- Orally rehearse stories and check that elements of the writer's hints are incorporated
- Finalise plan

Phase 2 outcome
To have planned my sequel

PHASE 3

- Shared write opening to get the writing process started
- Children independently write the opening and build up paragraphs
- Mark and follow-up on issues before they move onto the problem and resolution parts
- Shared write /children independently write problem, resolution and ending
- Support them to edit and refine story
- Publish, share and evaluate

UNIT PLANS

Quest by Aaron Becker

Instructions
How to complete a quest; how to complete a part of the quest; how to free a captured king; how to cross a rope bridge; how to make a rainbow

Explanation
How the crayons came to be where they are; guide to looking after a rhinoceros; how an airship works; rainbows; how the rainbow saved the king

Narrative
Write the Quest story; the story of the king's capture; the story of the quest map; innovate the story by changing the escape from each place

Description
The palace setting; the quest map; places on the quest map, e.g. underwater ruin, island palace, rope bridge; flying

USING PICTURE BOOKS AS HOOKS 75

UNIT PLAN	
Theme: **Quest** – Explanation	Key Stage 2

FINAL OUTCOME
Write an explanation of how to look after a rhinoceros

PHASE 1

- Re-read *Quest* and read a made up letter from the children in *Quest* asking for help with looking after their rhinoceros
- Shared read explanation texts (e.g. How bees make honey; how hot air balloons fly; The Teacher Pleaser Machine by Pie Corbett)
- Explore, respond and identify audience and purpose of each
- Review any design aspects that are particularly useful for readers, e.g. diagrams
- Collect effective vocabulary/language of explanations
- Chunk an explanation text into parts so that children understand the structure (introduction, explanation of aspects, conclusion)
- Create a list of writer's hints for this type of explanation text

Phase 1 outcome
To know what a good explanation looks and sounds like

PHASE 2

- Use a combination of books, film and drama to support children to gather ideas on how to look after a rhinoceros (bearing in mind the purpose and audience for their writing)
- Introduce new technical vocabulary and play talk games for children to orally rehearse
- Use text chunked in phase 1 to help plan it
- Provide opportunities for children to share and orally rehearse their ideas
- Finalise plans

Phase 2 outcome
To have planned my explanation

PHASE 3

- Shared write introductory paragraph —model how to use plan
- Children independently write the introduction
- Mark and follow-up on issues before they move onto the main body of the explanation
- Shared write to support with main body and concluding paragraphs
- Children independently write rest of explanation
- Support them to edit and refine whole text
- Add additional aspects such as diagrams
- Publish, share and evaluate

UNIT PLAN

Theme: *Quest* – Instructions　　　　　　　　　　　　　　　　　　　　**Key Stage 2**

FINAL OUTCOME
Write instructions for how to complete a quest

PHASE 1

- Explain task – to write a set of instructions on completing a quest
- Re-read *Quest*, asking children to take notes as if they have to instruct someone on completing a quest
- Shared read various sets of instructions
- Explore and respond; compare & contrast
- Identify the features and typical language of instructions (e.g. introduction, what you need, what you do, imperative verbs, ordered steps, concluding statement)
- Collect writer's hints for instructions
- Play language games to develop understanding of the use of precise vocabulary and of detailed steps within instructions
- Chunk text into sections and discuss layout (refer to purpose and audience)

Phase 1 outcome
To know what a good set of Instructions looks and sounds like

PHASE 2

- Using the 'what you do' section as a starting point for planning begin to orally rehearse and then plan each step
- Use talk activities to support with ideas for adding detail into each step
- Based on what is in the 'what you do' section, discuss what you might put into the 'what you need' section. Add to plan
- Use talk activities to support with ideas for what you might put into an introduction and a conclusion
- Complete plan

Phase 2 outcome
To have planned my instructions

PHASE 3

- Shared write introduction
- Children write introduction and 'what you need' independently
- Mark, feedback and follow-up on issues before moving on
- Shared write first part of steps
- Children write steps independently
- Mark, feedback and follow-up on issues before moving on
- Shared write concluding statement
- Children complete independently
- Mark, feedback and edit
- Publish, share and evaluate

USING PICTURE BOOKS AS HOOKS

	UNIT PLAN	
Theme: *Quest* – Narrative		Key Stage 2

FINAL OUTCOME:
To write the *Quest* story

PHASE 1

- Hook – using a visualiser (or similar device) shared read *Quest*
- Discuss the key events and focus on how the author has brought these to life
- Shared read a range of quest stories and respond
- Collect language & vocabulary that are effective
- Collect list of writer's hints for a good quest story
- Use the quest map to support with chunking *Quest* into events – break *Quest* down and check children understand each part

Phase 1 outcome
To know what a good quest story looks and sounds like

PHASE 2

- Show children mock up of *Quest* book
- Use the plot structure identified in phase 1 to begin to plan ideas; start with the story opening
- Discuss ideas and add to plan
- Discuss, orally rehearse and plan each part of the quest, incorporating effective vocabulary and language collected in phase 1
- Orally rehearse ideas and plan story ending
- Support children to plan how they will incorporate elements on the writer's hints list
- Finalise plan

Phase 2 outcome
To have planned my *Quest* story

PHASE 3

- Shared write opening to get the writing process started
- Children independently write the opening and next two paragraphs
- Mark and follow-up on issues before they move onto the next parts
- Shared write /children independently write next parts
- Mark and follow-up on issues before they move onto story ending
- Shared write /children independently write endings
- Support them to edit and refine story
- Publish, share and evaluate

UNIT PLANS

Sir Lancelot's First Quest from *King Arthur and the Knights of the Round Table* Retold by Marcia Williams

Information
Dragons; types of Dragon; Dragon Protection League Information leaflet; famous knights; Sir Lancelot; magicians; Excalibur; famous rescues; Magical Town travel brochure entry

Discussion
Witches are more powerful than knights; should dragon slaying be banned? legends are based on fact; It's better to be strong than clever

Narrative
Sir Lancelot's second quest; innovate the quests; set in the modern day; change the setting; re-write with more detail and with dialogue

Persuasion
Quest Job Advert; application to do a quest; Magical town trip advisor entry; Dragon Protection League campaign leaflet; Stop hunting dragons poster

UNIT PLAN

Theme: *Sir Lancelot's First Quest* – Discussion

Key Stage 2

FINAL OUTCOME
To write a discussion – Should Dragon Slaying Be Banned?

PHASE 1

- Read a range of discussion texts
- Explore purpose and audience for each; agree basic principles of these kinds of discussions
- Use talk activities to further explore the concept of 'discussion'
- Collect list of writer's hints
- Collect discursive language
- Play language games to practise using discursive language
- Chunk a discursive text into sections to clarify structure of discussion texts (Introduction, points for, points against, conclusion)

Phase 1 outcome
To know what good discussion texts look and sound like

PHASE 2

- Hooks – 1. Re-read *Sir Lancelot's First Quest* 2. Read a notice from King Arthur asking for views on whether he should ban dragon slaying
- Introduce the task: To write a discussion about whether dragon slaying should be banned
- Use chunks from phase 1 to start to plan new discussion
- Use hot-seating, role-play and discussion based activities to explore arguments for and against
- Use language games to further explore the effective use of discursive language and weave this through the arguments already established
- Complete plan

Phase 2 outcome
To have planned my own discussion text

PHASE 3

- Shared write introduction and points for paragraph/s
- Children independently write introduction and points for paragraph/s
- Mark and follow-up on issues before they move on
- Shared write points against and concluding paragraphs
- Children independently write points against and concluding paragraphs
- Mark and follow-up on issues
- Support with editing and refining discussions
- Share and evaluate (including relating back to initial hook)

UNIT PLAN

Theme: *Sir Lancelot's First Quest* – Narrative Key Stage 2

FINAL OUTCOME
To re-write *Sir Lancelot's First Quest* with more detail and dialogue

PHASE 1

- Explain task
- Re-read *Sir Lancelot's First Quest*
- Share out the 9 sections of the story and ask each group to discuss 1. what detail could they add 2. what dialogue could be added
- Use drama to try out the groups' ideas
- Shared read other short quest stories and draw out how detail and dialogue have both been used effectively
- Direct teach about dialogue and effective use of dialogue (if necessary)
- Create a blank planner of the 9 story sections

Phase 1 outcome
To know how to use detail and dialogue for effect

PHASE 2

- Using the blank planner, begin to plan ideas; start with the story opening
- Discuss ideas and add to plan
- Discuss, orally rehearse and plan each part of the story, thinking throughout about adding detail and where dialogue would work well
- Practise the language of written dialogue
- Discuss ideas for the story ending and add to plan
- Finalise plan

Phase 2 outcome
To have planned my story

PHASE 3

- Shared write opening
- Children independently write the opening
- Mark and follow-up on issues before they move onto the next parts
- Shared write /children independently write next parts, concentrating on adding detail and appropriate dialogue
- Mark and follow-up on issues before they move onto story ending
- Shared write /children independently write endings
- Support them to edit and refine story
- Publish, share and evaluate

USING PICTURE BOOKS AS HOOKS 81

UNIT PLAN

Theme: *Sir Lancelot's First Quest* – Persuasion

Key Stage 2

FINAL OUTCOME
To write persuasive information and reviews about the magical town (in the style of Trip Advisor)

PHASE 1

- Re-read *Sir Lancelot's First Quest* and discuss the setting: Do you think it would be a good place to visit? Why? Why not?
- Explain task. Discuss who might be interested in visiting the magical town and why (establish audience for information text)
- Choose a city or place and shared read about it on the Trip Advisor website
- Explore all of the information provided, e.g. places to stay, things to do
- Now read the reviews (you will need to vet these first!)
- Immerse the children in Trip Advisor style information
- Collect writer's hints for a Trip Advisor information piece
- Collect and bank new vocabulary and language
- Chunk a typical information page to get a feel for structure

Phase 1 outcome
To understand the Trip Advisor style of persuasive information and reviews

PHASE 2

- Using the illustrations in *Sir Lancelot's First Quest*, support children to develop ideas for what they would include in their information page
- Begin to plan, using chunks from phase 1
- Play word and language games to support with the use of persuasive information
- Orally rehearse — support with development
- Finalise plan (bear in mind audience and purpose)
- Provide opportunities for children to consider what the reviews of the magical town might include

Phase 2 outcome
To have planned my persuasive information piece

PHASE 3

- Shared write a short persuasive information piece to get the writing process started
- Children write theirs independently
- Mark, feedback and edit/refine
- Shared write two or three short reviews
- Children write a few short reviews
- Mark, feedback and edit/refine
- Evaluate

UNIT PLANS

Storm Whale
by
Sarah Brennan

Information
Whales; dolphins; sea/ocean; beach/coast; famous rescues; Save the Whales; Greenpeace

Discussion
Should humans interfere with nature? Should humans eat whale meat? Should whales be used for entertainment? Seaside living is better than city living

Narrative
Change from first person and re-tell the story; add to and re-tell parts of the story; tell from the whale's viewpoint; Write another whale or dolphin story; rescue story

Description
Collect descriptive language from Storm Whale, find synonyms, write new descriptions; Collect verbs from Storm Whale, find synonyms, use in new sentences; Sea/beach setting descriptions; animal descriptions

UNIT PLAN

Theme: *Storm Whale* – Description & Action **Key Stage 2**

FINAL OUTCOME
To write setting descriptions and action paragraphs

PHASE 1

- Read *Storm Whale* – perform it!
- Select the best sections for children to learn by heart and perform (the purpose of this is to internalise the language)
- Use drama and role-play to bring those sections to life and enable the children to understand them
- Bank the new vocabulary, explore meanings and collect synonyms for key adjectives and verbs
- Provide opportunities for children to generate sentences and paragraphs using the new vocabulary
- Share, discuss and evaluate in order to understand effective language use
- Chunk a description to get a feel for structure
- Chunk an action paragraph to get a feel for structure

Phase 1 outcome
To know what good descriptions and action paragraphs sound like

PHASE 2

- Decide on theme for descriptions, e.g. stormy weather, the sea and share stimuli with children (photographs, film clips etc.)
- Generate and bank vocabulary
- Orally rehearse including bringing in vocabulary collected in phase 1
- Decide on theme for action paragraph, e.g. running down busy streets, struggling through dense forest and share stimuli with children (photographs, film clips etc.)
- Generate and bank vocabulary
- Orally rehearse including bringing in vocabulary collected in phase 1

Phase 2 outcome
To have orally rehearsed my description and action paragraphs

PHASE 3

Carry out the following process for both pieces of writing:
- Short shared write to get children started
- Children write independently
- Mark and feedback; children edit and refine
- Children read their writing aloud, they themselves and others evaluate

UNIT PLAN

Theme: *Storm Whale* – Discussion

Key Stage 2

FINAL OUTCOME
To write a discussion – Should humans interfere with nature?

PHASE 1

- Read a range of discussion texts (factual rather than persuasive and emotive)
- Explore purpose and audience for each; agree basic principles of these kinds of discussions
- Use talk activities to further explore the concept of 'discussion'
- Collect list of writer's hints
- Play language games to practise using discursive language
- Chunk a discursive text into sections to clarify structure of discussion texts (Introduction, points for, points against, conclusion)

Phase 1 outcome
To know what good discussion texts look and sound like

PHASE 2

- Hooks – 1. Re-read *Storm Whale* 2. Read news article on David Attenborough interfering with nature during filming 'Dynasties'
- Introduce the task: To write a discussion about whether humans should interfere with nature
- Use chunks from phase 1 to start to plan new discussion
- Use research and discussion based activities to explore arguments for and against
- Use language games to further explore the effective use of discursive language and weave this through the arguments already established
- Complete plan

Phase 2 outcome
To have planned my own discussion text

PHASE 3

- Shared write introduction and points for paragraph/s
- Children independently write introduction and points for paragraph/s
- Mark and follow-up on issues before they move on
- Shared write points against and concluding paragraphs
- Children independently write points against and concluding paragraphs
- Mark and follow-up on issues
- Support with editing and refining discussions
- Share and evaluate (including relating back to initial hook)

UNIT PLAN

Theme: *Storm Whale* – Narrative   Key Stage 2

FINAL OUTCOME
To write a story in a sea or seaside setting

PHASE 1

- Re-read *Storm Whale* and explain task
- Shared read stories in a similar setting and collect themes, e.g. pirates, sea monsters, shipwrecks
- Select one story that grips the children and re-read
- Collect language & vocabulary that are effective
- Chunk the basic plot into sections so that children understand it
- Collect list of writer's hints for this type of story

Phase 1 outcome
To know what a good sea-themed story looks and sounds like (plot & language)

PHASE 2

- Use drama to explore ideas for a new story set on or beside the sea
- Use the plot structure identified in phase 1 to begin to plan ideas
- Use oral rehearsal and further drama activities to develop ideas around the key events
- Plan main events, ending, and opening
- Support children to plan how they will incorporate elements on the writer's hints list
- Finalise plan

Phase 2 outcome
To have planned my story

PHASE 3

- Shared write opening to get the writing process started
- Children independently write the opening and build up paragraphs
- Mark and follow-up on issues before they move onto the problem and resolution parts
- Shared write to support, where necessary
- Children independently write rest of the story
- Support them to edit and refine the story
- Share and evaluate

Information
Day and night; about the dark; night time road safety; road cat's eyes; shadows; light; eyes; electricity; fear

Explanation
How Laszlo stopped being afraid of the dark; why people are afraid of the dark; what is electricity? How light bulbs work; how shadows are formed; light/dark investigations

The Dark by Lemony Snicket

Narrative
Innovate: The Thunder; The Lightning; The Wind; change the ending; change the character and the setting

Description
Darkness; dark places; night time; Laszlo's house; wind; storm; thunder; lightning; inside/outside; fear

USING PICTURE BOOKS AS HOOKS

UNIT PLAN

Theme: *The Dark* – Explanation   Key Stage 2

FINAL OUTCOME:
Write an explanation of what electricity is

PHASE 1

- Hook - Read *The Dark*
- Explain the task
- Shared read scientific explanation texts
- Explore and respond; identify audience, purpose of each and how this affects the tone and form
- Collect effective vocabulary/language of explanations
- Chunk a simple explanation text into parts so that children understand the structure (introduction, main explanation, conclusion)
- Create a list of writer's hints

Phase 1 outcome
To know what a good explanation looks and sounds like

PHASE 2

- Use a variety of sources to support children to research 'what is electricity?'
- Introduce new technical vocabulary and play talk games for children to orally rehearse
- Use text chunked in phase 1 to support with planning
- Provide opportunities for children to share and orally rehearse their ideas
- Check planning against writer's hints and add to plan
- Finalise plans

Phase 2 outcome
To have planned my explanation

PHASE 3

- Shared write introduction of explanation – model how to use plan
- Children independently write the introduction
- Mark and follow-up on issues before they move onto the main body of the explanation
- Shared write to support with main body and conclusion
- Children independently write rest of explanation
- Support them to edit and refine whole text
- Publish, share and evaluate

UNIT PLAN

Theme: *The Dark* – Information Key Stage 2

FINAL OUTCOME
Wikipedia entry on Cat's Eyes (road)

PHASE 1

- Shared read a variety of information texts (including on-line texts)
- Compare and contrast; explore and respond – likes, dislikes, puzzles, patterns
- Identify purpose & audience of each and how the form and tone reflect this
- Immerse the children in information texts so that they internalise the language patterns
- Collect effective language and vocabulary
- Collect writer's hints
- Chunk Wiki page into sections to analyse structure, check understanding of purpose of each section

Phase 1 outcome
I know what a good information page looks and sounds like

PHASE 2

- Hook – Watch short information film about road Cat's Eyes
- Re-watch it, ask children to take notes
- Discuss what Cat's Eyes are, how they came about etc
- Use word and language games to check understanding of technical vocabulary; and of the language appropriate to this type of information text
- Support children to create a plan using the chunks identified in phase 1: introduction. Orally rehearse/discuss what might be in the introduction
- Support children to plan other sections; orally rehearse to test out
- Support children to think about how you might conclude the text. Orally rehearse ideas. Add these to plan
- Consider layout – children to know what their page will look like

Phase 2 outcome
I have planned my information page

PHASE 3

- Shared write introduction – model how to use plan
- Children independently write the introduction
- Mark and follow-up on issues before they move onto the main body of the information page
- Shared write to support with main body and conclusion
- Children independently write rest of information page
- Mark and follow-up on issues
- Support them to edit and refine whole text
- Publish and evaluate

USING PICTURE BOOKS AS HOOKS 89

UNIT PLAN

Theme: *The Dark* – Narrative

Key Stage 2

FINAL OUTCOME
Write a new story – The Lightning

PHASE 1

- Shared read stories on the theme of fears
- Respond and discuss; compare and contrast; which is better and why?
- Read and respond to *The Dark*
- Use drama to explore the story, checking that children understand the key parts
- Support them to create a storyboard illustrating the key parts
- Chunk *The Dark* into sections to support with planning in phase 2
- Collect hints — what makes this a good story?

Phase 1 outcome
To know what a good fear story looks and sounds like

PHASE 2

- Explain task
- Discuss fears, e.g. dark, thunder, monsters and list the kinds of things people are afraid of
- Focus on lightning and collect ideas for why people might be afraid of it
- Using the chunks established in phase 1, begin to plan new story
- Use talk activities to explore new ideas
- Orally rehearse and add to plan
- Finalise plan

Phase 2 outcome
To have planned my story

PHASE 3

- Brief shared write to get children started
- Children independently write the first paragraphs
- Mark and follow-up on issues before they move onto the other parts
- Shared write to support, where necessary
- Children independently write rest of the story
- Support them to edit and refine the story
- Publish, share and evaluate

The Egg by M.P. Robertson

Description
George; dragon; travelling on a dragon; the dragon's home; contrasting settings

Explanation
How to care for a dragon; fire and how to breathe it; how to distress a damsel; the fine art of flying; how to hatch an egg; the lifecycle of a dragon; how the egg got into the chicken coop

Narrative
Prequel (the Egg's story); sequel (another George & the dragon story); change the animal; change the middle and ending

Recount
George's diary; dragon's diary; news recount; letter from dragon to George about his new life; letter from George to a friend about the dragon events

UNIT PLAN

Theme: *The Egg* – Explanation Lower Key Stage 2

FINAL OUTCOME
Write an explanation of how to distress a damsel or how to breathe fire

PHASE 1

- Re-read *The Egg* and stop at the parts where George is teaching the dragon new skills
- Explain that the children are going to write an explanation which is to help someone needing to teach a dragon
- Shared read explanation texts (e.g. How bees make honey; how hot air balloons fly; The Teacher Pleaser Machine by Pie Corbett)
- Explore and respond – likes, dislikes, puzzles, patterns; and identify audience and purpose of each
- Collect effective vocabulary/language of explanations
- Write a model explanation text 'The fine art of flying' and shared read it
- Chunk it into parts so that children understand the structure (introduction, chronological explanation how, conclusion)
- Create a list of writer's hints

Phase 1 outcome
To know what a good explanation looks and sounds like

PHASE 2

- Use a combination of books, film and drama to support children to gather ideas on how to distress a damsel or how to breathe fire
- Introduce new technical vocabulary and play talk games for children to orally rehearse
- Once children have chosen the explanation that they want to write, use text chunked in phase 1 to help plan it
- Provide opportunities for children to share and orally rehearse their ideas
- Finalise plans

Phase 2 outcome
To have planned my explanation

PHASE 3

- Shared write opening of explanation – model how to use plan
- Children independently write the opening
- Mark and follow-up on issues before they move onto the main body of the explanation
- Shared write to support with main body and closing
- Children independently write rest of explanation
- Support them to edit and refine whole text
- Publish, share and evaluate

UNIT PLAN

Theme: *The Egg* – Narrative

Lower Key Stage 2

FINAL OUTCOME
Write a new George and the Dragon adventure story

PHASE 1

- Read *The Egg* & discuss the characters: does George like adventures? What kind? What about the dragon?
- Shared read adventure stories
- Explore, respond and compare – likes, dislikes, puzzles, patterns
- Explore new vocabulary and bank it
- Create a story mountain or map of a typical adventure story; discuss the plot
- Children create a story mountain for another adventure story; check they understand plot
- Collect list of writer's hints for these stories

Phase 1 outcome
To know what a good adventure story sounds like and understand the plot

PHASE 2

- Use drama and role-play to generate ideas for a new adventure for George and the dragon
- Begin to create a new map, mountain or storyboard of the main events
- Discuss where the story might be set and whether other characters are involved
- Add to map or storyboard, then transfer to a plan
- Use word/language games to explore new vocabulary
- Orally rehearse new ideas
- Finalise plan

Phase 2 outcome
To have planned my story

PHASE 3

- Show children mock-up of final book
- Model write opening using plan
- Children write opening independently
- Model write main events using plan
- Children write main events independently
- Model write ending using plan
- Children write ending independently
- Mark, feedback and edit
- Publish, share and evaluate

UNIT PLAN	
Theme: *The Egg* – Recount Letter	Lower Key Stage 2

FINAL OUTCOME
Write a letter from the dragon to George

PHASE 1

- Write a model recount letter, perhaps from *George* to the dragon, shared read it and ask for the children's responses
- Explore and shared read other recounts
- Discuss purpose and audience for recounts, and how the tone and vocabulary of each changes according to purpose and audience
- Play with the sentence structures and vocabulary in the model so that children are clear about this text-type
- Chunk the model into key events – build a bank of transferrable vocabulary for each, and develop children's understanding of this vocabulary
- Use the model to explore tone and form for a re-count letter
- Collect writer's hints for this type of recount

Phase 1 outcome
To know what a good informal recount letter sounds like

PHASE 2

- Re-read *The Egg* and discuss where the dragon might be now? What is it doing? How does it pass the time?
- Explain the task to the children which is to reply to George in role as the dragon
- Support the children to build a plan of the dragon's recount, adding detail that would appeal to George
- Orally rehearse ideas, collecting and enhancing vocabulary
- Finalise plan

Phase 2 outcome
To have planned my letter

PHASE 3

- Shared write opening
- Children write opening independently
- Shared write middle sections
- Children write middle sections independently
- Edit and re-draft as necessary
- Shared write endings
- Children write endings independently
- Mark, feedback and polish drafts
- Publish, share and evaluate

UNIT PLANS

The Elephant's Friend Retold by Marcia Williams

Persuasion
One-sided argument: elephants shouldn't be kept in captivity; letter persuading the merchant to return the dog; the king's proclamation; 'companion for elephant' job advert

Explanation
How to look after an elephant; how to care for a pet; letter explaining why the dog should return; how the dog came to be an elephant's friend; how the dog returned

Narrative
Innovate the story: change the characters, change the setting; a new adventure for the elephant or the dog; write the dog's story

Information
Indian animals; pets; healthy eating; India; Ancient India; Folk Tales; Tales from around the world; Animal Tales; Sacred animals

USING PICTURE BOOKS AS HOOKS 95

UNIT PLAN
Theme: *The Elephant's Friend* – Information Text

Lower Key Stage 2

FINAL OUTCOME
Report on Elephants

PHASE 1

- Hook – Watch short film clips about elephants
- Explain task – invent purpose and decide on audience
- Immerse children in the text type by reading and analysing reports on animals. For each, discuss purpose and audience
- Chunk a report, e.g. from a double page spread in children's reference book, to establish the structure of a report
- Identify key features and collect effective language and vocabulary
- Discuss most effective layout
- Collect writer's hints

Phase 1 outcome
I know what a good information report looks and sounds like

PHASE 2

- Using chunked report from phase 1, decide on the key topics in the main body of the report, e.g. types of elephant, diet, habitats, families, communication
- Begin to create plan
- Support children to transfer research into meaningful chunks of information
- Orally rehearse use of appropriate and effective language
- Orally rehearse opening and concluding paragraph ideas
- Support children to make design decisions: what will their report look like on the page? Are they going to add any pictures? Where will they go? Why?
- Finalise plan

Phase 2 outcome
I have planned my report

PHASE 3

- Shared write introduction
- Children independently write introductions
- Mark, and support children to edit and refine
- Shared write main sections
- Children independently write main sections
- Mark, and support children to edit and refine
- Shared write conclusion
- Children independently write conclusions
- Mark, and support children to edit and refine and to check for impact on reader
- Add design elements
- Publish, share and evaluate

UNIT PLAN

Theme: *The Elephant's Friend* – Narrative   Lower Key Stage 2

FINAL OUTCOME:
Write The _____'s Friend story

PHASE 1

- Read *The Elephant's Friend* story & respond (likes, dislikes, puzzles, patterns)
- Break the story down to check children's comprehension of the plot
- Chunk it into sections so that children can see the structure of the story
- Collect effective vocabulary and language – check understanding of effect
- Build list of writer's hints

Phase 1 outcome
To know *The Elephant's Friend* story and what makes it a good story

PHASE 2

- Explain task – to write a new version with changed characters and setting
- Generate ideas for new characters and bank them
- Generate ideas for new settings linked to characters
- Use drama/role-play to explore main events of new stories
- Collect vocabulary along the way
- Map or plan new _____ Friend story
- Use word/language games to orally rehearse new vocabulary and language
- Orally rehearse new story
- Finalise plan

Phase 2 outcome
To have planned my story

PHASE 3

- Show children mock up of book
- Model write opening using plan
- Children write opening independently
- Model write main events using plan
- Children write main events independently
- Model write ending using plan
- Children write ending independently
- Mark, feedback and edit
- Publish and share

UNIT PLAN

Theme: *The Elephant's Friend* – Persuasion   Lower Key Stage 2

FINAL OUTCOME
The king's proclamation requesting the return of the dog

PHASE 1

- Re-read *The Elephant's Friend* up to the king's proclamation. Ask what the children think a proclamation is
- Hook – Write and shared read a proclamation, e.g. Prince trying out glass slipper (Cinderella); Giant offering reward for return of golden goose (Jack & the Beanstalk)
- Explain task
- Re-read model proclamation and discuss purpose, audience and tone (should be formal and flowery as well a persuasive!)
- Shared read other formal persuasive pieces
- Identify use of language, collect effective language and vocabulary
- Build list of writer's hints for a persuasive proclamation
- Chunk the model into parts to support children to understand how they could structure a proclamation

Phase 1 outcome
I know what a good, formal persuasive piece sounds like

PHASE 2

- Explore ideas for what the king's proclamation might say
- Group ideas into themes and generate persuasive sentences – orally rehearse to check that they are formal, sound right and have the right effect
- Use chunks from phase 1 to plan the proclamation

Phase 2 outcome
I have planned my proclamation

PHASE 3

- Shared write opening of proclamation
- Children independently write their proclamations
- Support them to edit and refine whole text
- Publish, share and evaluate

UNIT PLANS

The Ice Bear by Jackie Morris

Information
Author/illustrator study of Jackie Morris; Polar bears; Polar animals; Polar lands; Inuit people; Adaptation; Totem animals

Persuasion
One-sided argument: In The Ice Bear the raven is a troublemaker; Polar bears should not live in zoos; Campaign leaflet against global warming; speech for living with the bears; speech for living with the humans

Narrative
Flashback story; Arctic fox and owl are the parents' totem animals, write their stories; write a winter story for the Ice Bear to tell the boy; write a summer story for a parent to tell the boy; use a double page spread illustration as stimulus for a new story

Description
Select extracts to study the use of language, perform then invent sentences in the style of the author; landscapes; animals; habitats; homes

UNIT PLAN

Theme: *The Ice Bear* – Information Upper Key Stage 2

FINAL OUTCOME
Information text on Inuit people

PHASE 1

- Shared read a variety of information texts, including ones related to people and places
- Compare & contrast; explore & respond
- Identify purpose & audience of each and how the tone and form relate to the purpose and audience
- Collect writer's hints for what makes a good information text
- Chunk a text into sections to establish the structure of an information text
- Identify key features to add to writer's hints and collect language
- Play word & language games to practise and develop the language of the text type
- Introduce task: to write an information text about Inuit people

Phase 1 outcome
I know what a good information text looks and sounds like

PHASE 2

- Re-read *The Ice Bear*, stopping to explore the illustrations of the people, where they live, what they wear etc.
- Support children to research the topic using a variety of sources (film/internet etc.), keep it focussed, e.g. their homes, what they eat, what they wear
- Support children to develop a plan: 4 key sections; orally rehearse/discuss content of each section (using aspects from writer's hints list to make sure that it's as effective as possible)
- Support children to plan the introduction and conclusion

Phase 2 outcome
I have planned my information text

PHASE 3

- Shared write introductory paragraph
- Children independently write introductory paragraph
- Edit and refine
- In turn shared write, children independently write, edit and refine next 4 sections
- Shared/Independently write conclusion
- Refine to check for impact on reader
- Evaluate

UNIT PLAN

Theme: *The Ice Bear* – Narrative
Upper Key Stage 2

FINAL OUTCOME
To write a flashback story – the boy telling his story (as a grown man)

PHASE 1

- Read a range of short stories with flashbacks
- Explore purpose and audience for each
- Explore likes, dislikes, puzzles, patterns for each
- Use mapping to identify typical plot structure to these types of stories, and where the flashback sits, e.g. flashback/opening, build up, problem, resolution, ending OR opening, build up, flashback...
- Check that children are clear about how flashback is used to best effect – explore this if necessary – using language games
- Collect writer's hints – hat makes a good flashback story

Phase 1 outcome
To know what a good flashback story sounds like

PHASE 2

- Explain the task and then read *The Ice Bear*
- Read again, asking the children to note down the key events that they would include if they were telling the story in the first person
- Use drama and role-play to guide thinking through 1. main events 2. how characters might feel & react
- Create individual plans
- Use drama to add to ideas around action/dialogue
- Focus on the flashback part; support children to gather ideas and then orally rehearse
- Check against writer's hints
- Finalise plans

Phase 2 outcome
To have planned my flashback story

PHASE 3

- Brief shared writing opening to model expectations
- Children independently write the first two sections of the story
- Mark and follow-up on issues before they move onto the next parts
- Shared write to support, where necessary – especially the flashback part
- Children independently write rest of the story
- Support them to edit and refine the story
- Publish, share and evaluate

USING PICTURE BOOKS AS HOOKS

UNIT PLAN

Theme: *The Ice Bear* – Persuasion   Upper Key Stage 2

FINAL OUTCOME
Persuasive speech – live with the bears OR live with humans

PHASE 1

- Re-Read *The Ice Bear* and stop at the part where the boy has to choose where he lives
- Discuss how the boy might be feeling at this point; do a quick conscience alley activity to see what the children would have chosen if it were them
- Hook – write a letter from the boy stating that the arrangement of half a year with each isn't working and asking the children to help him to decide where to live
- Explain task: to write a speech persuading the boy either to live with the bears or with the humans
- Listen to and shared read persuasive speeches
- Compare and contrast – which works best and why?
- Identify the tone of each and how this relates to audience
- Identify use of language, collect and check understanding of what makes it effective
- Collect list of writer's hints for persuasive speeches
- Chunk a persuasive speech into sections to help children understand structure

Phase 1 outcome
I know what a good persuasive speech sounds like

PHASE 2

- Use drama/role-play to explore the arguments that you might put for living with the bears and living with the humans
- Group ideas into themes and generate persuasive sentences – orally rehearse to check that they sound right and have the right effect
- Ensure children choose what their speech is about and then use chunks from phase 1 to plan
- Take elements from the list of hints and practise using them as part of the arguments
- Orally rehearse each section
- Add vocabulary to plan
- Finalise plan

Phase 2 outcome
I have planned my persuasive speech

PHASE 3

- Shared write speech introduction
- Children independently write their introduction
- Mark and follow-up on issues before they move onto the main body of the speech
- Shared write to support with main body and conclusion
- Children independently write rest of speech
- Support them to edit and refine whole text – oral rehearsal is important here
- In small groups, children perform their speeches; each group chooses the best one (against writer's hints list)
- Children evaluate each other's speeches
- 6 best speeches are performed to class

The Tin Forest by Helen Ward & Wayne Anderson

Recount
Old man's diary/journal; magazine article about the changes to the Tin Forest or about the old man's life; letters to/from the old man

Explanation
How we can affect climate change; how to care for our environment; the lifecycle of plants and requirements for life; why humans need plants; how to reduce, reuse, recycle

Narrative
Innovate: The Plastic Forest; The Plastic Sea; turn into a wordless picture book and write a new story to match the illustrations; write a story about change; prequel; flashback story, from old man's viewpoint

Persuasion
Climate change based one-sided argument or leaflet: switch off lights; save water; reduce, reuse, recycle; walking is the best way to travel; conservation adverts/posters

USING PICTURE BOOKS AS HOOKS 103

UNIT PLAN

Theme: *The Tin Forest* – Narrative Key Stage 2

FINAL OUTCOME
To write a flashback story – the old man telling his version of the story

PHASE 1
- Read a range of short stories with flashbacks
- Explore likes, dislikes, puzzles, patterns for each
- Discuss typical plot structure to these types of stories, and where the flashback sits, e.g. flashback/opening, build up, problem, resolution, ending OR opening, build up, flashback...
- Collect writer's hints – what makes a good flashback story
- Explain the task and then re-read *The Tin Forest*
- Chunk the story into key events, including where the setting will need to be described
- Collect vocabulary and language that children can use in their stories

Phase 1 outcome
To know what a good flashback story sounds like and know *The Tin Forest*

PHASE 2
- Use drama and role-play to guide thinking through how the old man might feel & react to each key event
- Discuss how the setting changes; play language games to support children's knowledge of appropriate vocabulary to be used
- Create individual plans
- Focus on the flashback part; support children to gather ideas and then orally rehearse
- Check against writer's hints
- Finalise plans

Phase 2 outcome
To have planned my flashback story

PHASE 3
- Brief shared writing opening to model expectations
- Children independently write the first two sections of the story
- Mark and follow-up on issues before they move onto the next parts
- Shared write to support, where necessary – especially the flashback part
- Children independently write rest of the story
- Mark and follow-up on issues; support them to edit and refine the story
- Publish, share and evaluate

UNIT PLAN

Theme: *The Tin Forest* – Persuasion
Key Stage 2

FINAL OUTCOME
Write a one-sided argument – walking is the best way to travel

PHASE 1

- Re-visit the environmental issues discussed as a result of reading and discussing *The Tin Forest*
- Hook – NHS (UK) has a 'Walk to Work Day' as one of their health and wellbeing campaigns; share information on this and discuss
- Explain task: to write a one-sided argument entitled 'Walking is the best way to travel'
- Shared read one-sided argument texts
- Compare and contrast – which works best and why?
- Identify the tone of each and how this relates to audience
- Identify use of language, collect and check understanding of what makes it effective
- Collect list of writer's hints for one-sided arguments
- Chunk a one-sided argument text into sections to help children understand structure (introduction, 2/3 paragraphs each with a main point and explanation/justification, conclusion)

Phase 1 outcome
I know what a good one-sided argument text looks and sounds like

PHASE 2

- Ascertain who the audience might be for such a text
- Use drama/role-play to explore the arguments that you might put for walking instead of using modes of transport
- Group ideas into themes and generate persuasive sentences – orally rehearse to check that they sound right and have the right effect
- Use chunks from phase 1 to plan, start with main points
- Generate ideas and plan introductions and conclusions
- Take elements from the list of hints and practise using them as part of the arguments
- Orally rehearse each section
- Add vocabulary to plan
- Check planned ideas are appropriate to audience
- Finalise plan

Phase 2 outcome
I have planned my one-sided argument text

PHASE 3

- Shared write introduction
- Children independently write their introduction
- Mark and follow-up on issues before they move onto the main parts
- Shared write to support with main parts
- Children independently write main parts
- Mark and follow-up on issues before they move onto the conclusion
- Shared write conclusion
- Children independently write their conclusion
- Mark and follow-up on issues; support with editing and refining
- Share and evaluate

UNIT PLAN

Theme: *The Tin Forest* – Recount (diary)   Key Stage 2

FINAL OUTCOME
Write the old man's diary entries

PHASE 1

- Shared read diary entries/extracts (avoid ones that are too informal – remember that these are models for writing)
- Compare & contrast; explore & respond – likes, dislikes, puzzles, patterns; and identify purpose of each, e.g. logging major events
- Build a list of writer's hints for diaries (avoid an over emphasis on informal language)
- Chunk a diary entry into parts to support with structure
- Hook – re-read *The Tin Forest*

Phase 1 outcome
To know what a good diary entry sounds like

PHASE 2

- Support the children to think through when the old man might have written in his diary and about what
- Hot seat him to establish how he felt at key moments and other details
- Plan using the chunks from phase 1 as a structure
- Collect vocabulary (including time connectives to structure the recount)
- Play word/language games to orally rehearse the use of time words and the use of vocabulary to add detail – children add these to their plan
- Follow the same process again for different events so that children have several diary entries planned

Phase 2 outcome
To have planned my diary entries

PHASE 3

Carry out the following process for each diary entry:
- Shared write a diary entry – model how to use plan
- Children independently write their own entry
- Mark and follow-up on issues before they move onto the next diary entry
- Model write if necessary
- Children independently write rest of diary entries
- Support them to edit and refine as they go along
- Publish, share and evaluate

UNIT PLANS

Information
Story book wolves; The Big Bad Wolf; wolves; farm animals; materials; forces; predators; keeping safe

Discussion
Are storybook wolves bad? Should Big Bad Wolf be sent to prison? Should Big Bad Wolf become a vegetarian? Are traditional tales entertaining? Do traditional tales have hidden messages?

The True Story of the 3 Little Pigs by Jon Scieszka

Narrative
The true story from a pig's point of view; The true story of another traditional tale, e.g. Goldilocks or Little Red Riding Hood; Twist on 3 Little Pigs, e.g. one of the pigs is the baddie

Recount
News recount; the pigs' eye witness accounts; police reports about the events (wolf's and pigs'); a pig's letter about the events to his mum; wolf's letter to his friend

USING PICTURE BOOKS AS HOOKS

UNIT PLAN
Theme: *The True Story of the 3 Little Pigs* – Discussion   Key Stage 2

FINAL OUTCOME
Write a discussion – Should A. Wolf go to prison?

PHASE 1

- Shared read a range of discussion texts
- Explore purpose and audience for each
- Use talk activities to further explore the concept of discussion
- Collect list of writer's hints for writing a discussion
- Play language games to practise using discursive language
- Chunk a discursive text into sections to clarify structure of discussion texts (paragraphs: introduction, points for, points against, conclusion)

Phase 1 outcome
To know what a good discussion text looks and sounds like

PHASE 2

- Re-read *The True Story of the 3 Little Pigs*
- Introduce task: Discussion 'should A. Wolf go to prison?' Hold an initial class discussion on this
- Use discussion based role-play and drama games, e.g. conscience alley, to explore points for and against
- Use chunks from phase 1 to help to plan new discussion
- Use language games to practise the effective use of discursive language, and other aspects on the writer's hints list
- Orally rehearse possible introductions/conclusions to this discussion
- Complete plan

Phase 2 outcome
To have planned my own discussion text

PHASE 3

- Shared write introduction and points for paragraph
- Children independently write introduction and points for paragraph
- Shared write points against and concluding paragraphs
- Children independently write points against and concluding paragraphs
- Support with editing and refining discussions
- Share and evaluate
- Publish

UNIT PLAN
Theme: *The True Story of the 3 Little Pigs* – Information
Key Stage 2

FINAL OUTCOME
Wiki page on Story Book Wolves

PHASE 1
- Shared read a variety of information texts (ideally about topics such as animals, book characters, living things)
- Compare & contrast; explore & respond – likes, dislikes, puzzles, patterns; and identify purpose & audience of each
- Collect writer's hints for information texts
- Study some Wiki pages and add to writer's hints (what makes a good Wiki page?)
- Collect effective language and vocabulary
- Chunk a Wiki page into sections to analyse structure, check understanding of purpose of each section

Phase 1 outcome
I know what a good information page looks and sounds like

PHASE 2
- Referring to *The True Story of the 3 Little Pigs*, explain the task
- Discuss who the audience might be for this writing
- Provide books and picture prompts to support children to consider what they could write about story book wolves
- Use chunks from phase 1 to start to plan the Wiki page
- Use talk activities to support with the development, and oral rehearsal, of ideas for each section of the plan
- Finalise plan
- Consider design aspects – how will they lay out their page? Will they add any photographs? Extra text?

Phase 2 outcome
I have planned my information page

PHASE 3
- Shared write opening section
- Children independently write opening section
- Mark and support children to edit, refine and evaluate
- Shared write other sections, where necessary
- Children independently write other sections
- Edit and refine to check for impact on reader
- Add design elements
- Publish, share and evaluate

UNIT PLAN
Theme: *The True Story of the 3 Little Pigs* – Narrative   Key Stage 2

FINAL OUTCOME
Write The True Story of Goldilocks (or other)

PHASE 1
- Read *The True Story of the 3 Little Pigs*, discuss & respond
- Map or storyboard key moments of *The True Story of the 3 Little Pigs*
- Then explore viewpoint & how Jon Scieszka has portrayed the wolf at key moments of the story
- Collect list of writer's hints for writing a story from a different point of view
- Discuss other traditional tales with wolves in them; what do you think those wolves are like?
- If they could tell The True Story of... what would they say?

Phase 1 outcome
To know *The True Story of the 3 Little Pigs* and understand writing from a different viewpoint

PHASE 2
- Continue to explore other traditional tales and how they could be written from a different viewpoint
- Support children to select a story to write The True Story of (recommend Goldilocks)
- Model how to plan their True Story
- Orally rehearse new ideas
- Share and check out new ideas; add to plan
- Finalise plan

Phase 2 outcome
To have planned my story

PHASE 3
- Show children mock – up of final book
- Model write opening using plan
- Children write opening independently
- Model write main events using plan
- Children write main events independently
- Model write ending using plan
- Children write ending independently
- Mark, feedback and edit

Using novels and short stories as hooks

Mind maps and unit plans

UNIT PLANS

Great Sharp Scissors by Philippa Pearce (From Lion at School and Other Stories)

Persuasion
Argument: Tim was naughty; Mum shouldn't have left Tim home alone; advert's for: sharp Scissors; spray-on Glue; Granny's jam

Recount
Tim's letter to granny; Mum's account of leaving Tim home alone; Tim's diary

Narrative
Innovate the story by changing: what he cut; what he bought to fix and then mend things; new Great Sharp Scissors story with new characters and setting; new Great Sharp xxx story

Instructions
Tim's rules for staying home alone; How to use Great Sharp Scissors; How to use Spray-on Glue; Jam making

USING NOVELS AND SHORT STORIES AS HOOKS 115

UNIT PLAN	
Theme: *The Great Sharp Scissors* – Narrative	Key Stage 1

FINAL OUTCOME
Write a new *Great Sharp Scissors* Story

PHASE 1

- Read *The Great Sharp Scissors* story & respond (likes, dislikes, puzzles, patterns)
- Break the story down to check children's comprehension of the plot
- Chunk it into sections so that children can see the structure of the story
- Collect effective vocabulary and language – check understanding of effect
- Build list of writer's hints

Phase 1 outcome
To know *The Great Sharp Scissors* story and what makes it a good story

PHASE 2

- Discuss ways to change the characters and setting to create a new story
- Use drama/role-play to explore how a version of the story might work with different characters and in a different setting
- Collect vocabulary along the way
- Map or plan new *Great Sharp Scissors* story
- Orally rehearse new story
- Finalise plan

Phase 2 outcome
To have planned my story

PHASE 3

- Model write opening using plan
- Children write opening independently
- Mark, feedback and follow-up on issues throughout writing process
- Model write main events using plan
- Children write main events independently
- Model write ending using plan
- Children write ending independently
- Mark, feedback and edit
- Publish and share

UNIT PLAN
Theme: *The Great Sharp Scissors* – Persuasion (Advert)
Key Stage 1

FINAL OUTCOME
Adverts for spray-on glue (TV and/or on-line)

PHASE 1

- Hook – watch TV adverts around a theme, e.g. household helpers, gadgets
- Shared read on-line adverts on the same theme
- General discussion re adverts – Purpose? Audience?
- Collect effective vocabulary and language structures
- Collect synonyms
- Discuss any relevant design features (that children may use on their own adverts)
- Re-read the part of *The Great Sharp Scissors* story that has spray-on glue
- Explain task

Phase 1 outcome
I know what persuasion is and what a good persuasive advert looks and sounds like

PHASE 2

- Gather ideas for what might be included in an advert for spray-on glue, e.g. possible uses, possible audience
- Model and support children to plan their advert/s
- If planning TV adverts use drama to help children to explore what they might say
- Introduce the vocabulary collected at phase 1 - orally rehearse using this as part of the persuasion
- Finalise plans

Phase 2 outcome
I have planned my advert/s

PHASE 3

- Shared write advert/s to get children started
- Independent & guided write adverts
- Share, evaluate and re-draft to ensure message is clear
- Make final design decisions
- Publish and evaluate for overall impact

USING NOVELS AND SHORT STORIES AS HOOKS 117

UNIT PLAN

Theme: *The Great Sharp Scissors* – Recount   Key Stage 1

FINAL OUTCOME
Tim's recount letter to granny

PHASE 1

- Write and shared read a model recount letter from granny to Tim
- Shared read other recount letters
- Clarify what a recount is and discuss purpose and audience for recounts
- Play with the sentence structures and vocabulary in the model so that children are clear about this text-type
- Chunk the model into key events – use this to support knowledge of structure and explore the use of time connectives
- Build a bank of vocabulary and develop children's understanding of this vocabulary; explore synonyms and alternative phrases
- Collect writer's hints for a recount letter (include awareness of audience)

Phase 1 outcome
To know what a good recount letter looks and sounds like

PHASE 2

- Explain task (to reply to granny as if you are Tim)
- Read *The Great Sharp Scissors* and chunk the events from the point of view of Tim
- Discuss each event; what would Tim say about each? What would he say to granny? Explore tone as well as content
- Using the chunks from phase 1, build a plan of Tim's recount letter, adding detail that takes the audience (granny) into account
- Orally rehearse, collecting and enhancing vocabulary
- Finalise plan

Phase 2 outcome
To have planned my recount letter

PHASE 3

- Shared write opening
- Children write opening independently
- Shared write middle sections
- Children write middle sections independently
- Edit and re-draft as necessary
- Shared write endings
- Children write endings independently
- Mark, feedback and polish drafts
- Publish, share and evaluate (perhaps you could send them to granny and see if she replies!)

UNIT PLANS

***Lion at School* by Philippa Pearce**
(From Lion at School and Other Stories)

Explanation
How to ride on a lion; keeping a wild animal at school; how to care for a lion; how to feed a lion; how to get your school dinner

Description
Lions; teachers; familiar settings; Jack Tall; Betty Small

Narrative
Innovate the story by changing: the lion; characters; setting; write another adventure for: the lion; Betty Small; Jack tall

Information
Lions; pets; unusual lion related events; unusual school related events; school dinners menu; lion's dinner menu

UNIT PLAN

Theme: *Lion at School* – Description

Key Stage 1

FINAL OUTCOME
Wild animal descriptions

PHASE 1

- Hook – read a description of an animal and ask the children to listen carefully and identify the animal
- Shared read a variety of descriptions about animals
- Compare and contrast – which are effective and why?
- Collect descriptive language and vocabulary
- Identify the structure of a typical description of an animal
- Collect writer's hints

Phase 1 outcome
To know what a good animal description sounds like

PHASE 2

- Explain task
- Use picture and film stimulus to generate vocabulary to describe a lion (or other chosen wild animal)
- Play word/language games to develop vocabulary and the language of description
- Focus on the way that the animal moves, chases and catches its prey etc. and bank vocabulary and language for this
- Shared plan animal descriptions
- Pair work – children 'talk' their descriptions
- Finalise plans

Phase 2 outcome
To have planned my animal description

PHASE 3

- Model write first couple of lines (including modelling how to work from a plan)
- Children independently write their descriptions
- Mark/feedback, edit and refine
- Provide stimulus for different wild animal; children plan and independently write a second description (putting into practice what they have learned from the first)
- Mark, feedback edit, refine, and publish

UNIT PLAN

Theme: *Lion at School* – Explanation
Key Stage 1

FINAL OUTCOME
Write an explanation of how to keep a lion at school

PHASE 1

- Play talk games to establish what an explanation is, for example, explain how you got to school this morning, explain what makes day and night
- Shared read simple explanation texts
- Explore and respond – likes, dislikes, puzzles, patterns; and identify audience and purpose of each
- Immerse children in explanation texts so that they know the typical language patterns
- Collect effective vocabulary/language of explanations
- Chunk a simple explanation text into parts so that children understand the structure (introduction, chronological explanation of how/why, conclusion)
- Create a list of writer's hints

Phase 1 outcome
To know what a good explanation looks and sounds like

PHASE 2

- Re-visit *Lion at School* and discuss what Noil does at school and how Betty Small looks after him
- Explain task – imagine Betty is writing this to help other children
- Generate ideas around keeping a lion at school, the school day and what Betty might need to say
- Introduce new technical vocabulary and play talk games for children to orally rehearse
- Use text chunked in phase 1 to help plan new explanation
- Orally rehearse ideas and the language of explanation
- Finalise plan

Phase 2 outcome
To have planned my explanation

PHASE 3

- Show children a mock-up of final explanation i.e. how it could be laid out on the page
- Shared write opening of explanation – model how to use plan
- Children independently write the opening
- Mark and follow-up on issues before they move onto the main body of the explanation
- Shared write to support with main body and closing
- Children independently write rest of explanation
- Support them to edit and refine whole text
- Publish, share and evaluate

USING NOVELS AND SHORT STORIES AS HOOKS

UNIT PLAN	
Theme: *Lion at School* – Narrative	Key Stage 1

FINAL OUTCOME
New adventure for Betty Small

PHASE 1

- Read Lion at School & respond
- Break the story down to check children's comprehension of the plot
- Use a story map or mountain so that children can see the structure of the story
- Investigate Betty Small's character, e.g. hot seat her, identify what type of person she is by what she does and says etc.
- Imagine a back-story for her, e.g. does she have siblings, is she a good friend?

Phase 1 outcome
To know the *Lion at School* story and know about Betty Small

PHASE 2

- Explain task – write a new Betty Small story
- Explore and collect children's ideas for what might happen in a new Betty Small story
- Map or plan the story
- Use drama to check out ideas and orally rehearse
- Use word/language games to orally rehearse new vocabulary and language
- Clarify ideas for how the story will end
- Finalise plan

Phase 2 outcome
To have planned my story

PHASE 3

- Model write opening using plan
- Children write opening independently
- Mark, feedback and follow-up on issues throughout writing process
- Model write main events using plan
- Children write main events independently
- Model write ending using plan
- Children write ending independently
- Mark, feedback, and edit
- Publish and share

UNIT PLAN

Theme: *Little Lord Feather-Frock* – Persuasion

Key Stage 1

FINAL OUTCOME
Apology letter from Old Foxy

PHASE 1

- Hook – write a model apology letter from a book character, e.g., from The Gruffalo, Goldilocks, The Big Bad Wolf, and read to the children
- Discuss purpose and audience; explain that this type of text is 'persuasive'
- Shared read *Little Lord Feather-Frock* and introduce task: To write an apology letter to the characters in role as Old Foxy
- Use drama to establish what Old Foxy might say in his letter
- Collect effective vocabulary and language structures
- Chunk the model letter into sections so that children understand how it is structured
- Collect list of writer's hints for persuasive letters

Phase 1 outcome
I know what persuasion is and what a good persuasive letter looks and sounds like

PHASE 2

- Drawing on the language and ideas collected at phase 1, support the children to plan their letter
- Orally rehearse the letters using elements from the writer's hints
- Develop the children's ideas so that they (Old Foxy) have lots to say
- Finalise plan

Phase 2 outcome
I have planned my letter

PHASE 3

- Shared write opening of letter – model how to use plan
- Children independently write the opening
- Mark and follow-up on issues before they move onto the main body of the letter
- Shared write to support with main body and closing
- Children independently write rest of letter
- Support them to edit and refine whole text
- Publish, share and evaluate
- Send letters to the characters!

USING NOVELS AND SHORT STORIES AS HOOKS 125

UNIT PLAN	
Theme: *Little Lord Feather-Frock* – Recount	Key Stage 1

FINAL OUTCOME
Old Foxy's Diary

PHASE 1

- Write a model Old Foxy diary entry about the rooster's first near miss
- Discuss purpose and audience for diaries and explain that they are recounts
- Shared read other diary entries
- Play with the sentence structures and vocabulary in the model so that children are clear about this text-type
- Use the model to support knowledge of structure and explore the use of time connectives
- Collect writer's hints for a diary entry

Phase 1 outcome
To know what a good diary entry looks and sounds like

PHASE 2

- Re-read the rest of *Little Lord Feather-Frock*
- Discuss each event; what would Old Foxy say about each?
- Build a new plan of Old Foxy's diary entries
- Orally rehearse, collecting and enhancing vocabulary
- Finalise plans

Phase 2 outcome
To have planned my diary entries

PHASE 3

- Shared write opening of first entry to get the writing going
- Children write first entry independently
- Mark, feedback, edit and re-draft
- Children write second entry independently (putting into practice what they have learned from the first)
- Mark, feedback and polish
- Publish, share and evaluate

UNIT PLANS

Mr Majeika by Humphrey Carpenter

Explanation
How to: Be a wizard; make vampire teeth disappear; keep your mouth clean; Hamish's guide to rule dodging; Mr Majeika's guide to magic powers; rules for new teachers

Recount
Biography of Mr Majeika; Mr Majeika's life as a wizard; flying; recount of Hamish being a frog; the day we turned the classroom into a fairytale palace

Narrative
Short story: With Mr Majeika in a different setting; Mr Majeika turns someone into something and can't turn them back; innovate how he does magic; re-write what happens when Mr Potter drinks the flying potion

Instructions
Teachers' Magic Spells; Mr Majeika's Spells; flying potion

USING NOVELS AND SHORT STORIES AS HOOKS

UNIT PLAN

Theme: *Mr Majeika* – Explanation
Key Stage 1

FINAL OUTCOME
Write an explanation of how to be a wizard

PHASE 1

- Play talk games to establish what an explanation is, e.g. explain how you got to school this morning, explain what makes day and night
- Shared read simple explanation texts
- Explore and respond – likes, dislikes, puzzles, patterns; and identify audience and purpose of each
- Immerse children in explanation texts so that they know the typical language patterns
- Collect effective vocabulary/language of explanations
- Chunk a simple explanation text into parts so that children understand the structure (introduction, chronological explanation of how/why, conclusion)
- Create a list of writer's hints

Phase 1 outcome
To know what a good explanation looks and sounds like

PHASE 2

- Re-visit extracts from *Mr Majeika* and discuss what makes him a wizard and what his powers are
- Explain task – imagine *Mr Majeika* is writing this to help people who want to be wizards
- Generate ideas around wizard powers, behaviours and what *Mr Majeika* might need to say
- Introduce new technical vocabulary and play talk games for children to orally rehearse
- Use text chunked in phase 1 to help plan new explanation
- Orally rehearse ideas and the language of explanation
- Finalise plan

Phase 2 outcome
To have planned my explanation

PHASE 3

- Show children a mock-up of final explanation i.e. how it could be laid out on the page
- Shared write opening of explanation – model how to use plan
- Children independently write the opening
- Mark and follow-up on issues before they move onto the main body of the explanation
- Shared write to support with main body and closing
- Children independently write rest of explanation
- Support them to edit and refine whole text
- Publish, share and evaluate

UNIT PLAN

Theme: *Mr Majeika* – Instructions
Key Stage 1

FINAL OUTCOME
Write a set of instructions on Teachers' Magic Spells

PHASE 1

- Re-read an extract from *Mr Majeika* that includes one of his spells, e.g. turning a ruler into a snake or Hamish into a frog, and then explain task
- Shared read various sets of instructions
- Explore and respond – compare & contrast
- Identify the features and typical language of instructions (e.g. introduction, what you need, what you do, imperative verbs, ordered steps, concluding statement)
- Check children understand the chunks of instructions (introduction, what you need, what you do, conclusion)
- Build list of writer's hints for instructions

Phase 1 outcome
To know what a good set of Instructions looks and sounds like

PHASE 2

- Play games that involve the children giving instructions to each other
- Draw out the language and continue to build banks and understanding
- Generate ideas for what a new teacher spell could be for
- Use chunked set of instructions as basis for plan of new set
- Practise use of imperative verbs appropriate to their instructions
- Talk activities to support with ideas for what you might put into an introduction, and the 'what you need' section
- Talk activities to support with ideas for adding detail into each step
- Support with ideas for a concluding statement
- Complete plan

Phase 2 outcome
To have planned my instructions

PHASE 3

- Shared write introduction
- Children write introduction and 'what you need' independently
- Shared write initial steps
- Children write steps independently
- Mark, feedback and follow-up on issues throughout writing process
- Shared write concluding statement
- Children complete independently
- Mark, feedback and edit
- Publish and share

USING NOVELS AND SHORT STORIES AS HOOKS

UNIT PLAN

Theme: *Mr Majeika* – Narrative

Key Stage 1

FINAL OUTCOME
Write a new event for the *Mr Majeika* Story

PHASE 1

- Re-cap the part of the novel where *Mr Majeika* turned Hamish Bigmore into a frog and couldn't turn him back into a human
- Discuss what the children liked about this part and why it was effective
- Break this event down into parts so that children can see the structure, e.g. Hamish is naughty, *Mr Majeika* turns him into a frog etc.
- Discuss other events in the novel and use these to build a list of writer's hints for what makes a good story

Phase 1 outcome
To know the story and what makes it a good story

PHASE 2

- Explain task – to write a new event in which *Mr Majeika* turns a pupil into something and can't turn them back
- Use drama/role-play to explore new ideas
- Using structure collected at phase 1 map or plan new *Mr Majeika* event
- Orally rehearse new story
- Collect and build new vocabulary to express ideas
- Check ideas against list of writer's hints
- Finalise plan

Phase 2 outcome
To have planned my story

PHASE 3

- Model write opening using plan
- Children write opening independently
- Mark, feedback and follow-up on issues throughout writing process
- Model write main events using plan
- Children write main events independently
- Model write ending using plan
- Children write ending independently
- Mark, feedback and edit
- Publish and share

UNIT PLANS

Mrs Pepperpot has a visitor from America by Alf Prøysen (From Mrs Pepperpot Stories)

Persuasion
Rules: What to do when you shrink: how to treat Mrs Pepperpot if you see her; One-sided argument: Being shrunk is more fun than being regular size; adverts for jobs you can do if you're shrunk

Recount
Thank you letter from Mrs Pepperpot's sister; diary entries: Mrs Pepperpot; her diary from when she was young; her sister's diary

Narrative
Innovate the story by setting it in your town/city; change where the sisters meet, what she buys etc.; write a new Mrs Pepperpot adventure that involves her shrinking

Information
About Mrs Pepperpot; guide to living with Mrs Pepperpot; famous small book characters, for example, Tom Thumb, Tinkerbell; famous giants, e.g. smartest Giant in Town, The BFG

USING NOVELS AND SHORT STORIES AS HOOKS 131

UNIT PLAN
Theme: *Mrs Pepperpot has a visitor from America* – Information   Key Stage 1

FINAL OUTCOME
To write a Wiki page about famous book characters that are small

PHASE 1
- Read a range of internet information pages
- Explore and respond – which do you prefer and why? Purpose and audience of each?
- Identify information page features
- Immerse children in information pages about people and film/TV/book characters
- Identify the typical structure of a Wiki page about a famous person or character
- Collect and explore transferable vocabulary
- Collect list of writer's hints for information pages

Phase 1 outcome
To know what a good Wiki page looks and sounds like

PHASE 2
- Explain task
- Explore famous book characters that are small, e.g. Tom Thumb, Tinkerbell, The Borrowers
- Support children to decide on the information that they will include in their own page
- Plan Wiki page
- Collect and build relevant vocabulary
- Orally rehearse ideas
- Refine and/or develop them
- Finalise plan

Phase 2 outcome
To have planned my Wiki page

PHASE 3
- Model how to use plan to write introduction, and shared write
- Independent write of introductions
- Model how to use plan to write next part of information page, and shared write
- Independent write of next parts
- Re-draft elements that need polishing
- Add visuals, e.g. photographs
- Publish, share and evaluate

UNIT PLAN

Theme: *Mrs Pepperpot has a visitor from America* – Narrative   Key Stage 1

FINAL OUTCOME
Write a new adventure for Mrs Pepperpot

PHASE 1

- Read *Mrs Pepperpot has a visitor from America* & respond
- Discuss Mrs Pepperpot's character – her name, characteristics, when she shrinks etc.
- Break the story down to check children's comprehension of the plot
- Use a story map or mountain so that children can see the structure of the story, focussing on Mrs Pepperpot shrinking and returning to full size
- Collect writer's hints for when Mrs Pepperpot shrinks, e.g. shrinks when she is stressed, travels in a handbag

Phase 1 outcome
To know what makes the Mrs Pepperpot story good

PHASE 2

- Explain task – to write a new story in which Mrs Pepperpot shrinks
- Provide the setting and other characters as stimulus and then use drama/role-play to explore new ideas
- Using structure collected at phase 1 map or plan new Mrs Pepperpot story
- Orally rehearse new story
- Collect and build new vocabulary to express ideas
- Check ideas against list of writer's hints
- Finalise plan

Phase 2 outcome
To have planned my story

PHASE 3

- Model write opening using plan
- Children write opening independently
- Mark, feedback and follow-up on issues throughout writing process
- Model write main events using plan
- Children write main events independently
- Model write ending using plan
- Children write ending independently
- Mark, feedback and edit
- Publish and share

UNIT PLAN	
Theme: *Mrs Pepperpot has a visitor from America* – Persuasion	Key Stage 1

FINAL OUTCOME
Write a one-sided argument – why being shrunk is more fun than regular size

PHASE 1

- Hook – Write and share a letter from Mr Pepperpot asking the children to help cheer his wife up as she's fed up with shrinking (include arguments against shrunk being fun)
- Shared read model text and chunk so that children understand the structure (introduction, reasons why being shrunk is not fun, conclusion)
- Discuss the reasons and how these are structured (reason and explanation, e.g. It can be frightening: I might get stepped on, be eaten by a dog etc.)
- Create a list of writer's hints for an argument text
- Explain task – to write a letter to Mrs Pepperpot persuading her that being shrunk is fun

Phase 1 outcome
I know what a good one-sided argument text looks and sounds like

PHASE 2

- Re-read extracts from the story about Mrs Pepperpot being shrunk
- Discuss and collect ideas about why being shrunk is fun
- Use chunks from phase 1 to plan, start with main points
- Generate ideas and plan introductions and conclusions
- Take elements from the list of hints and practise using them as part of the arguments
- Orally rehearse each section
- Add vocabulary to plan
- Check planned ideas are appropriate
- Finalise plan

Phase 2 outcome
I have planned my one-sided argument text

PHASE 3

- Shared write opening – model how to use plan
- Children independently write the opening
- Mark and follow-up on issues before they move onto the main body
- Shared write to support with main body and closing
- Children independently write rest
- Support them to edit and refine whole text
- Publish, share and evaluate
- Send letters to Mrs Pepperpot!

UNIT PLAN
Theme: *Mrs Pepperpot's Birthday* – Instructions Key Stage 1

FINAL OUTCOME
Write a recipe (tea party item, e.g. strawberry layer cake)

PHASE 1
- Read *Mrs Pepperpot's Birthday*
- Ask the children if they've ever been to a tea party and discuss why, where, when?
- Show pictures of a typical tea party spread (perhaps mocked up to look like *Mrs Pepperpot's birthday* tea)
- Explain task: To write a set of instructions for making a birthday tea item (recipe)
- Shared read various sets of instructions and recipes
- Explore and respond – compare & contrast
- Identify the features and typical language of recipes (e.g. introduction, what you need, what you do, imperative verbs, ordered steps, concluding statement)
- Build list of writer's hints for recipes
- Discuss the layout of a recipe – look at real recipe books as well as on-screen. Decide on the best layout for your recipe writing.

Phase 1 outcome
To know what a recipe looks and sounds like

PHASE 2
- Support children to make the chosen item, take photographs as they do
- Use photographs to support with planning recipe writing
- Practise use of imperative verbs appropriate to this set of instructions
- Talk activities to support with ideas for what you might put into an introduction and conclusion
- Talk activities to support with ideas for adding detail into each step, e.g. stir in the icing sugar being careful to start slowly and increase speed
- Complete plan

Phase 2 outcome
To have planned my instructions

PHASE 3
- Shared write introduction
- Children write introduction and 'what you need' independently
- Mark and follow-up on issues throughout the writing process
- Shared write steps
- Children write steps independently
- Shared write concluding statement
- Children complete independently
- Mark, feedback and edit
- Publish and share

USING NOVELS AND SHORT STORIES AS HOOKS 137

UNIT PLAN
Theme: *Mrs Pepperpot's Birthday* – Narrative   Key Stage 1

FINAL OUTCOME
Write a new *Mrs Pepperpot's Birthday* story

PHASE 1
- Read *Mrs Pepperpot's Birthday* & respond (likes, dislikes, puzzles, patterns)
- Break the story down to check children's comprehension of the plot
- Chunk it into sections so that children can see the structure of the story
- Collect effective vocabulary and language – check understanding of effect
- Build list of writer's hints

Phase 1 outcome
To know *Mrs Pepperpot's Birthday* story and what makes it a good story

PHASE 2
- Discuss ways to change the characters who come to Mrs Pepperpot's birthday and what they bring
- Use drama/role-play to explore the new ideas
- Collect vocabulary along the way
- Map or plan new *Mrs Pepperpot's Birthday* story
- Orally rehearse new story
- Finalise plan

Phase 2 outcome
To have planned my story

PHASE 3
- Model write opening using plan
- Children write opening independently
- Mark, feedback and follow-up on issues throughout writing process
- Model write main events using plan
- Children write main events independently
- Model write ending using plan
- Children write ending independently
- Mark, feedback and edit
- Publish and share

UNIT PLANS

Peter and the Wolf
By Sergei Prokofiev

https://archive.org/details/PeterAndTheWolf_753
(Audio version)

Persuasion
Letter to the wolf persuading not to eat/chase/frighten other animals; wanted poster; persuasive argument: persuade hunters not to catch the wolf

Information
Instruments; orchestras; wolves; storybook wolves; predators; snowy places; prokofiev; famous composers

Narrative
Change characters; change who the wolf catches; change the wolf; change how the wolf is captured; once changed choose new musical/percussion instruments and perform; act out story with changed instruments/percussion

Explanation
How to catch a wolf; how to avoid a wolf; how a violin works; how a wind instrument works; how a drum works

USING NOVELS AND SHORT STORIES AS HOOKS 139

UNIT PLAN	
Theme: *Peter and the Wolf* – Explanation	Key Stage 1

FINAL OUTCOME
Write an explanation of how to catch a story-book wolf

PHASE 1

- Play talk games to establish what an explanation is, e.g. explain how you got to school this morning, explain what makes day and night
- Shared read simple explanation texts
- Explore and respond – likes, dislikes, puzzles, patterns; and identify audience and purpose of each
- Immerse children in explanation texts so that they know the typical language patterns
- Collect effective vocabulary/language of explanations
- Chunk a simple explanation text into parts so that children understand the structure (introduction, chronological explanation of how/why, conclusion)
- Create a list of writer's hints

Phase 1 outcome
To know what a good explanation looks and sounds like

PHASE 2

- Explain task
- Discuss story-book wolves: which stories the children know, whether the wolves are good or bad, how the bad ones are treated/punished etc.
- Generate ideas around explaining how to catch a wolf, including who the audience might be for such an explanation
- Introduce new technical vocabulary and play talk games for children to orally rehearse
- Use text chunked in phase 1 to help plan new explanation
- Orally rehearse ideas and the language of explanation
- Finalise plan

Phase 2 outcome
To have planned my explanation

PHASE 3

- Shared write opening of explanation – model how to use plan
- Children independently write the opening
- Mark and follow-up on issues before they move onto the main body of the explanation
- Shared write to support with main body and closing
- Children independently write rest of explanation
- Support them to edit and refine whole text
- Publish, share and evaluate

UNIT PLAN

Theme: *Peter and the Wolf* – Information   Key Stage 1

FINAL OUTCOME
To write fact-files about musical or percussion instruments

PHASE 1

- Shared read a range of information texts/fact-files
- Explore and respond – which do you prefer and why?
- Immerse the children in a range of fact-files
- Identify fact-file features
- Build up a list of writer's hints

Phase 1 outcome
To know what a good fact-file looks and sounds like

PHASE 2

- Listen to the audio version of *Peter and the Wolf*
- Hook – look at illustrations of the musical and percussion instruments used; discuss what children know about them
- Use children's knowledge and other sources to collect facts and vocabulary
- Plan two fact-files (including 'design' decisions)
- Orally rehearse ideas
- Refine and/or develop them

Phase 2 outcome
To have planned my fact-files

PHASE 3

- Model how to use plan and shared write first fact-file
- Children write their first fact-file
- Read and provide feedback
- Support children to edit and improve their fact-files
- Support children to write their second fact-file
- Feedback, edit and improve
- Publish

USING NOVELS AND SHORT STORIES AS HOOKS

UNIT PLAN

Theme: *Peter and the Wolf* – Narrative | Key Stage 1

FINAL OUTCOME
Write and perform an innovated *Peter and the Wolf* story

PHASE 1

- Listen to the audio version of *Peter and the Wolf*; identify the instruments/percussion used to symbolise the characters
- Share illustrations of *Peter and the Wolf* and discuss how the characters are portrayed
- Discuss Prokofiev's choice of sound for each character
- Chunk the story into sections so that children can see the structure of the story

Phase 1 outcome
To have heard the audio version of the story and know how sound represents characters

PHASE 2

- Generate ideas for which characters to change and who their replacements might be
- Use drama/role-play to explore how a version of the story might work with different characters
- Support the children to choose new characters for their story and select music/percussion to represent each of them
- Use a story map or board to plan the new story
- Orally rehearse new story ready for writing

Phase 2 outcome
To have planned my story

PHASE 3

- Model write to get writing started
- Children write their new version independently
- Mark, feedback and edit stories
- Share and evaluate
- Provide opportunities for children to orally rehearse a performance of their new story with instruments/percussion
- Perform

UNIT PLAN

Theme: *Rumpelstiltskin* – Recount Key Stage 1

FINAL OUTCOME
Girl Spins Straw into Gold news report for Castle Press

PHASE 1

- Shared read simple local news reports and respond (you may need to write your own simple model)
- Discuss purpose of news reports and audience for reports about local news
- Identify the language of recount within the reports and collect key vocabulary/language
- Chunk one of the reports into parts so that children understand the structure
- Agree what makes a good news report and collate a list of writer's hints

Phase 1 outcome
To know what a good news report looks and sounds like

PHASE 2

- Hook – mock up the front page of the Castle Press and ask the children what kinds of news might be reported in it
- Explain that they are going to write a news report about the girl spinning straw into gold
- Re-read relevant extracts from Rumpelstiltskin and use these to begin to plan the reports
- Use the chunks identified in phase 1 to support with structure
- Discuss each event and orally rehearse what you might say about it, using 'news' vocabulary and language collected at phase 1
- Finalise plan

Phase 2 outcome
To have planned my news report

PHASE 3

- Shared write opening
- Children write opening independently
- Shared write middle sections
- Children write middle sections independently
- Edit and re-draft as necessary
- Shared write endings
- Children write endings independently
- Mark, feedback and polish drafts
- Publish, share and evaluate

USING NOVELS AND SHORT STORIES AS HOOKS

UNIT PLAN

Theme: *Rumpelstiltskin* – Persuasion

Key Stage 1

FINAL OUTCOME
Letter from Ms Miller persuading her father, the miller, to rescue her

PHASE 1

- Hook – write a letter from Mr Miller to his daughter and shared read it
- Ask the children to respond; how do they think Ms Miller would respond?
- Agree that she would write back asking him to save her
- General discussion on what persuasion is and when we use it
- Shared read a model persuasive letter
- Discuss purpose and audience; is it an effective letter? Why?
- Identify use of language, collect effective language and vocabulary
- Chunk the letter into sections
- Build list of writer's hints for persuasive letters

Phase 1 outcome
I know what a good persuasive letter looks and sounds like

PHASE 2

- Support children to generate ideas for what Ms Miller might say to her father
- Use chunks from phase 1 to plan new letters
- Take elements from the list of hints and practise using them in the context of Ms Miller
- Orally rehearse each section of the letter
- Add vocabulary to plan
- Finalise plan

Phase 2 outcome
I have planned my persuasive letter

PHASE 3

- Shared write opening – model how to use plan
- Children independently write the opening
- Mark and follow-up on issues before they move onto the main body of the letter
- Shared write to support with main body and closing
- Children independently write rest of letter
- Support them to edit and refine whole text
- Publish, share and evaluate
- Send letters to Mr Miller and see if he replies!

UNIT PLANS

Information
Clothes making; sewing; re-cycling; upcycling; clothing banks; fairtrade; fairtrade cotton

Explanation
Where clothes come from; how buttons work; why upcycling is important; what happens to unwanted clothing; how recycling works

The Blue Coat
Retold by Hugh Lupton
(From The Story Tree)

Narrative
Innovate the story: Change the coat and all other things mother made; change the characters and the setting; plan a new story and turn it into a storyboard or cartoon strip

Instructions
How to make a: coat, waistcoat, hat, bowtie, button; how to upcycle clothing; how to upcycle furniture

UNIT PLAN

Theme: *The Blue Coat* – Information
Key Stage 1

FINAL OUTCOME
To write an information leaflet about recycling clothing

PHASE 1

- Read a range of information leaflets
- Explore and respond – which do you prefer and why? Purpose and audience of each?
- Identify information leaflet features (including visual elements such as pictures/diagrams)
- Chunk a leaflet into sections to support understanding of structure (introduction, sections of information, fascinating fact, conclusion)
- Collect and explore transferable vocabulary
- Collect list of writer's hints for information leaflets

Phase 1 outcome
To know what a good information leaflet looks and sounds like

PHASE 2

- Provide stimulus for new information leaflet (hook); could be a short film about landfill and the need to recycle more
- Decide on the information that the children will include in their own leaflet
- Using the chunks from phase 1, support children to plan leaflets (including 'design' decisions)
- Orally rehearse ideas
- Refine and/or develop them
- Develop and collect key vocabulary
- Check writer's hints are included
- Finalise plans

Phase 2 outcome
To have planned my information leaflet

PHASE 3

- Show children mock-up of a leaflet
- Model how to use plan to write introduction, and shared write
- Independent write of introductions
- Mark/feedback and children edit
- Model how to use plan to write next parts of leaflet, and shared write
- Independent write of next parts
- Model and write concluding parts
- Mark/feedback and children edit/polish
- Add visuals, e.g. photographs
- Publish, share and evaluate

UNIT PLAN	
Theme: *The Blue Coat* – Instructions	Key Stage 1

FINAL OUTCOME
Write instructions for how to make a waistcoat

PHASE 1

- Re-read *The Blue Coat* and discuss the pictures of Tom's mother making the clothes – do the children know anyone who makes clothes? Have they seen clothing being made?
- Explain task (instructions for making a doll-sized piece of clothing out of felt)
- Shared read various sets of instructions on this theme
- Explore and respond – compare & contrast
- Identify the features and typical language of instructions (e.g. introduction, what you need, what you do, imperative verbs, ordered steps, concluding statement)
- Build list of writer's hints for instructions

Phase 1 outcome
To know what instructions look and sound like

PHASE 2

- Support children to make the chosen item, take photographs as they do
- Use photographs to support with planning instruction writing
- Agree on audience for the instructions
- Practise use of imperative verbs appropriate to this set of instructions
- Talk activities to support with ideas for what you might put into an introduction and conclusion
- Talk activities to support with ideas for adding detail into each step, e.g. stitch neatly and carefully as they may be seen
- Complete plan

Phase 2 outcome
To have planned my instructions

PHASE 3

- Shared write introduction
- Children write introduction and 'what you need' independently
- Mark and follow-up on issues throughout the writing process
- Shared write steps
- Children write steps independently
- Shared write concluding statement
- Children complete independently
- Mark, feedback and edit
- Publish and share

USING NOVELS AND SHORT STORIES AS HOOKS 149

UNIT PLAN

Theme: *The Blue Coat* – Narrative
Key Stage 1

FINAL OUTCOME:
Write The Blue XX Story

PHASE 1

- Read *The Blue Coat* & respond (likes, dislikes, puzzles, patterns)
- Break the story down to check children's comprehension of the plot
- Chunk it into sections so that children can see the structure of the story
- Collect effective vocabulary and language – check understanding of effect
- Build list of writer's hints

Phase 1 outcome
To know *The Blue Coat* story and what makes it a good story

PHASE 2

- Explain the task
- Discuss what item of clothing could be used instead of a coat and what else this could be made into to create a new story
- Map or plan new The Blue XX (cape, jacket, trousers etc.) story
- Develop and collect related vocabulary
- Orally rehearse new story
- Finalise plan

Phase 2 outcome
To have planned my story

PHASE 3

- Model write opening using plan
- Children write opening independently
- Mark, feedback and follow-up on issues throughout writing process
- Model write main events using plan
- Children write main events independently
- Model write ending using plan
- Children write ending independently
- Mark, feedback and edit
- Publish and share

Persuasion
For each of the lands: trip advisor entries & reviews; adverts; dame snap's school prospectus; adverts for: moon face's magic powder; pop cakes; well-i-never rolls; lands to avoid

Explanation
Guide to: Each of the lands; leaving each of the lands; faraway tree; use of the slippery-slip; how to climb the Faraway Tree

The Enchanted Wood
By Enid Blyton

Narrative
Make up a new land and write an adventure in it; New adventure for a favourite character; stop at Chapter 27 write what happens to the Goblins; story of the Land of the Red Goblins; wishing cake story

Information
The Enchanted Wood; the faraway tree; any of the lands; the railway; giant-land; country of loneliness

UNIT PLAN

Theme: *The Enchanted Wood* – Explanation Key Stage 1

FINAL OUTCOME
Write a guide to the Faraway Tree

PHASE 1

- Play talk games to establish what an explanation is, e.g. explain how you got to school this morning, explain your school morning routine
- Shared read simple explanation texts, e.g. a guide to living in a tree house, guide to use of tree swings
- Explore and respond – likes, dislikes, puzzles, patterns; and identify audience and purpose of each
- Immerse children in explanation texts so that they know the typical language patterns
- Collect effective vocabulary/language of explanations
- Chunk a simple explanation text into parts so that children understand the structure (introduction, explanation of how/why/what, conclusion)
- Create a list of writer's hints

Phase 1 outcome
To know what a good explanation looks and sounds like

PHASE 2

- Explain task
- Re-visit extracts from *The Enchanted Wood* and discuss the Faraway Tree
- Discuss what might be included in a guide to the Faraway Tree and bank ideas
- Introduce new technical vocabulary and play talk games for children to orally rehearse
- Use text chunked in phase 1 to help plan new explanation
- Orally rehearse ideas and the language of explanation
- Finalise plan

Phase 2 outcome
To have planned my explanation

PHASE 3

- Show children a mock-up of final explanation i.e. how it could be laid out on the page
- Shared write opening of explanation – model how to use plan
- Children independently write the opening
- Mark and follow-up on issues before they move onto the main body of the explanation
- Shared write to support with main body and closing
- Children independently write rest of explanation
- Support them to edit and refine whole text
- Publish, share and evaluate

UNIT PLAN

Theme: *The Enchanted Wood* – Information Page

Key Stage 1

FINAL OUTCOME
To write an information page about *the Enchanted Wood*

PHASE 1

- Read a range of information texts
- Explore and respond – which do you prefer and why? Purpose and audience of each?
- Immerse children in information texts about places
- Identify information page features (including visual elements such as pictures/diagrams) and typical structure
- Collect and explore transferable vocabulary
- Collect list of writer's hints for information texts

Phase 1 outcome
To know what a good information page looks and sounds like

PHASE 2

- Hook—show children mock-up of a class book on *The Enchanted Wood*. Explain task
- Use extracts from the novel to explore *The Enchanted Wood*; support children to decide on the aspects that they would like to write about
- Collect and build relevant vocabulary and language (this should be of a non-narrative form and tone)
- Support children to plan their information pages
- Orally rehearse ideas
- Refine and/or develop them
- Finalise plan

Phase 2 outcome
To have planned my information page

PHASE 3

- Model how to use plan to write introduction, and shared write
- Independent write of introductions
- Model how to use plan to write next parts of information page, and shared write
- Independent write of next parts
- Re-draft elements that need polishing
- Add visuals, e.g. photographs
- Publish, share and evaluate

UNIT PLAN

Theme: *The Enchanted Wood* – Narrative   Key Stage 1

FINAL OUTCOME
Write a wishing cake story

PHASE 1

- Re-read the end of chapter 31 of *The Enchanted Wood* to remind children about the wishing cake
- Ask the children to imagine what the wishing cake might look like; where it might have come from; who made it etc.
- Explain the task and read/discuss other stories that have wishes in them that the children know, e.g. Magic Porridge Pot, A Squash and a Squeeze, Aladdin
- Use a map or mountain to plot the events of the wishing cake so that the children can see the structure
- Collect writer's hints about what makes a good wishing story

Phase 1 outcome
To know what makes a good wishing story

PHASE 2

- Support the children to decide whether they are going to set their new story in a fantasy world or in their own setting – explore ideas
- For their chosen setting, explore who the characters could be (guide the children towards choosing 3 characters)
- Using structure collected at phase 1 map or plan new wishing cake story
- Use drama/role-play to explore plot: what the wishes are, why they want them etc.
- Orally rehearse new story
- Check ideas against list of writer's hints
- Finalise plan

Phase 2 outcome
To have planned my story

PHASE 3

- Model write opening using plan
- Children write opening independently
- Mark, feedback and follow-up on issues throughout writing process
- Model write main events using plan
- Children write main events independently
- Model write ending using plan
- Children write ending independently
- Mark, feedback and edit
- Publish and share

UNIT PLANS

The Twits by Roald Dahl

Instructions
How to make bird pie; how to use balloons to fly; the Twits' Tricks; how to train monkeys; how to turn the Twits upside down; Mr Twit's beard care; Mrs Twit's glass eye

Recount
Diary entries about: the frog trick; Wormy spaghetti trick; shrinking Mrs Twit; turning the Twits upside down

Narrative
New short story about the Twits with new tricks; new short story in the style of The Twits; Descriptions: Twits' house and garden; The Twits; Muggle Wump; Roly Poly Bird

Information
Fact-files: Mr Twit; Mrs Twit; Muggle Wump; Roly Poly Bird; Birds

USING NOVELS AND SHORT STORIES AS HOOKS 155

UNIT PLAN	
Theme: *The Twits* – Information	Key Stage 1

FINAL OUTCOME
To write fact-files about Mr & Mrs Twit

PHASE 1

- Shared read a range of information texts/fact-files
- Explore and respond – which do you prefer and why?
- Immerse the children in a range of fact-files
- Identify fact-file features
- Build up a list of writer's hints

Phase 1 outcome
To know what a good fact-file looks and sounds like

PHASE 2

- Hook – look at illustrations of Mr and Mrs Twit
- Discuss and generate ideas for 'facts' about the Twits
- Explore key vocabulary
- Play word and language games to develop ideas,
- Plan two fact-files (including 'design' decisions)
- Orally rehearse ideas
- Refine and/or develop them

Phase 2 outcome
To have planned my fact-files

PHASE 3

- Model how to use plan and shared write first fact-file
- Children write their first fact-file
- Read and provide feedback
- Support children to edit and improve their fact-files
- Support children to write their second fact-file
- Feedback, edit and improve
- Publish

UNIT PLAN

Theme: *The Twits* – Instructions

Key Stage 1

FINAL OUTCOME
Write a set of instructions on one of the Twits' tricks

PHASE 1

- Re-read an extract from *The Twits* that includes one of the tricks and then explain task
- Shared read various sets of instructions
- Explore and respond – compare & contrast
- Identify the features and typical language of instructions (e.g. introduction, what you need, what you do, imperative verbs, ordered steps, concluding statement)
- Build list of writer's hints for instructions
- Play language games to develop understanding of imperative verb meanings, e.g. mime the action
- Check children understand the chunks of instructions (introduction, what you need, what you do, conclusion)

Phase 1 outcome
To know what a good set of Instructions looks and sounds like

PHASE 2

- Play games that involve the children giving instructions to each other
- Draw out the language and continue to build banks and understanding
- Use the novel to help the children to decide which trick their instructions are going to be about
- Use chunked set of instructions as basis for plan of new set
- Practise use of imperative verbs appropriate to their instructions
- Talk activities to support with ideas for what you might put into an introduction, and the 'what you need' section
- Talk activities to support with ideas for adding detail into each step, e.g. When they first feel the frog name a terrifying made up creature
- Support with ideas for a concluding statement
- Complete plan

Phase 2 outcome
To have planned my instructions

PHASE 3

- Shared write introduction
- Children write introduction and 'what you need' independently
- Shared write initial steps
- Children write steps independently
- Mark, feedback and follow-up on issues throughout writing process
- Shared write concluding statement
- Children complete independently
- Mark, feedback and edit
- Publish and share

USING NOVELS AND SHORT STORIES AS HOOKS 157

UNIT PLAN

Theme: *The Twits* – Narrative

Key Stage 1

FINAL OUTCOME:
Write a short story in the style of *The Twits*

PHASE 1

- Hook – find pictures of two funny characters; discuss them: Who are they? What's special about them? What kinds of things happen to them? etc.
- Explain task
- Use a story mountain to chunk a shortened version of the main events of *The Twits*
- Discuss what the children enjoyed about *The Twits* and collect writer's hints for what makes a good story of this type

Phase 1 outcome
To know what makes *The Twits* a good story

PHASE 2

- Using the story mountain as a guide, discuss the main events that will be included in your story (e.g. opening, a main event, ending)
- Discuss and bank ideas for what tricks the two characters will play on each other
- Now support the children to consider who the good character is and how they 'beat' the Twit type characters
- Orally rehearse ideas and put them into the story mountain planner
- Discuss how the children will end their stories
- Finalise plans

Phase 2 outcome
To have planned my story

PHASE 3

- Model write opening using plan
- Children write opening independently
- Model write main events using plan
- Children write main events independently
- Mark, feedback and follow-up on issues throughout the process
- Model write ending using plan
- Children write ending independently
- Mark, feedback and edit
- Publish, share and evaluate

Mind maps and unit plans

UNIT PLANS

The Brave Little Tailor
Retold by Philip Pullman
(From Grimm Tales for Young and Old)

Explanation
How to beat a giant; how to trick a king; how to tame a rhinoceros; how to be a story baddie; quests and how to succeed at them

Recount
Diary entries by: The tailor, a giant, a horseman, the princess; magazine article about the tailor becoming king

Narrative
Innovate opening: who he sees; what he takes with him; the king's quests; change the ending; write a Giants story, a Princess story, a new Brave Little Tailor story

Discussion
The tailor was brave; story giants are always gormless; the king was clever; story princesses are always clever; kings should choose husbands for their daughters

UNIT PLAN

Theme: *The Brave Little Tailor* – DiscussionKey Stage 2

FINAL OUTCOME
To write a discussion – Was the Little Tailor brave?

PHASE 1

- Read a range of discussion texts
- Explore purpose and audience for each; agree basic principles of these kinds of discussions
- Use talk activities to further explore the concept of 'discussion'
- Collect list of writer's hints
- Collect discursive language
- Play language games to practise using discursive language
- Chunk a discursive text into sections to clarify structure of discussion texts (Introduction, points for, points against, conclusion)

Phase 1 outcome
To know what good discussion texts look and sound like

PHASE 2

- Hook – explain the task and then carry out a short discussion on the topic (based on evidence from *The Brave Little Tailor*) followed by a class vote
- Using evidence from the novel, support children to discuss arguments for and against and collate ideas
- Use chunks from phase 1 to start to plan new discussion
- Use language games to further explore the effective use of discursive language and weave this through the arguments already established
- Support children to check plans against the writer's hints
- Complete plan

Phase 2 outcome
To have planned my own discussion text

PHASE 3

- Shared write introduction and points for paragraph/s
- Children independently write introduction and points for paragraph/s
- Mark and follow-up on issues before they move on
- Shared write points against and concluding paragraphs
- Children independently write points against and concluding paragraphs
- Mark and follow-up on issues
- Support with editing and refining discussions
- Share and evaluate
- Carry out a class vote, compare to original result!

UNIT PLAN

Theme: *The Brave Little Tailor* – Explanation

Key Stage 2

FINAL OUTCOME
Quests and how to succeed at them explanatory text

PHASE 1

- Shared read a variety of explanation texts
- Respond, identify audience and purpose of each and how the form and tone reflect the intended audience
- Collect effective vocabulary/language of explanations
- Review any design aspects that are particularly useful for readers, e.g. diagrams
- Chunk an explanation text into parts so that children understand the structure (introduction, explanation of aspects, conclusion)
- Create a list of writer's hints for explanation texts
- Explain task and discuss who the audience might be for such a text

Phase 1 outcome
To know what a good explanation looks and sounds like

PHASE 2

- Agree on the form and tone of the explanation text
- Use knowledge of quest stories and research to begin to plan the contents of the explanation
- Support children to plan the main body of the explanation
- Provide opportunities for children to share and orally rehearse their ideas
- Support children to plan their introductory paragraph/s and conclusion
- Finalise plans

Phase 2 outcome
To have planned my explanation

PHASE 3

- Shared write introductory paragraph — model how to use plan
- Children independently write the introduction
- Mark and follow-up on issues before they move onto the main body of the explanation
- Shared write to support with main body
- Children independently write main body
- Mark and follow-up on issues before moving onto the concluding paragraph
- Shared/independent write conclusion
- Support them to edit and refine whole text
- Add additional aspects such as diagrams
- Publish, share and evaluate

USING NOVELS AND SHORT STORIES AS HOOKS 163

UNIT PLAN

Theme: *The Brave Little Tailor* – Narrative   Key Stage 2

FINAL OUTCOME
To write a new Brave Little Tailor quest story

PHASE 1
- Hook – make up a hook into a new quest for *the Brave Little Tailor*, e.g. letter, video message, email
- Re-read *The Brave Little Tailor* asking the children to listen for the parts that involve a quest
- Discuss the different quests that the tailor completed
- Shared read a range of quest stories, respond (likes, dislikes, puzzles, patterns)
- Collect language & vocabulary that are effective
- Use a map or story mountain to outline the basic plot of a quest story
- Collect list of writer's hints

Phase 1 outcome
To know what a good quest story looks and sounds like

PHASE 2
- Support children to think about the new quest for the tailor — Who will set the quest? What might happen along the way? Who will she meet? Good? Evil? How will it end?
- Use talk activities and drama to add detail to 1. main events and 2. new characters
- Begin to plan ideas
- Orally rehearse main events using vocabulary and language collected at phase 1
- Support children to plan how they will incorporate elements of the writer's hints
- Finalise plan

Phase 2 outcome
To have planned my quest story

PHASE 3
- Shared write opening to get the writing process started
- Children independently write the opening and build up paragraphs
- Mark and follow-up on issues before they move onto the problem and resolution parts
- Shared write /children independently write problem, resolution and ending
- Support them to edit and refine story
- Publish, share and evaluate

UNIT PLANS

Cogheart by Peter Bunzl

Explanation
User's manual for mechanicals; Clockwork; how Cogheart works; how airships fly; how to drive an airship; Steam wagons; inventions; why mechanicals should have equal rights to humans; Zep highway code

Recount
Daily Cog news articles: Steam wagon accident, Mechs stolen, Mechs V Humans, Hartman missing

Narrative
New adventure for Malkin or Mrs Rust; Lily & Robert's Invention story; Penny dreadful stories; new story set in a sci-fi Victorian city; new story set in a sci-fi historical setting

Description
Characters: Lily, Malkin, Roach, Madame Verdigris, Mrs Rust, Anna Quinn; Settings: Brackenbridge, Brackenbridge Manor, Townsend's shop, Dragonfly crash scene, Ladybird zep, Behemoth zep

USING NOVELS AND SHORT STORIES AS HOOKS 165

UNIT PLAN
Theme: *Cogheart* – Character & Setting Descriptions   Key Stage 2

FINAL OUTCOME
To write a character and a setting description (Anna Quinn & Ladybird zep)

PHASE 1
- Explain tasks
- Shared read variety of good quality setting descriptions
- Collect writer's hints for setting descriptions
- Collect vocabulary and language
- Shared read variety of good quality character descriptions
- Collect writer's hints for character descriptions
- Collect vocabulary and language
- Explore the use of expanded noun phrases; metaphors, onomatopoeia, alliteration to add detail and effect
- Chunk each of a setting and a character description into parts so that children understand the structures

Phase 1 outcome
To know what good descriptions sound like

PHASE 2
- Re-read extracts from the novel that describe Anna and the Ladybird
- Collect and add vocabulary to the lists banked in phase 1
- Working on each description separately, support the children to create two plans
- Re-visit the text to develop ideas
- Support children to 'talk' their descriptions to orally rehearse and refine them
- Check ideas against writer's hints collected in phase 1
- Finalise plans

Phase 2 outcome
To have planned my descriptions

PHASE 3
Carry out the following process for both pieces of writing:
- Short shared write to get children started
- Children write independently
- Mark and feedback; children edit and refine
- Children read their writing aloud, they themselves and others evaluate

UNIT PLAN

Theme: *Cogheart* – Explanation   Key Stage 2

FINAL OUTCOME
Write a manual for a Mechanical Pet

PHASE 1

- Hook – read a made up letter from Malkin asking the children to write a manual for how to look after a mechanical pet
- Shared read explanation texts that focus on the theme of caring for/looking after animals
- Explore, respond and identify audience and purpose of each
- Review any design aspects that are particularly useful for readers, e.g. diagrams
- Collect effective vocabulary/language of explanations
- Chunk an explanation text into parts so that children understand the structure (introduction, explanation of aspects, conclusion)
- Create a list of writer's hints for this type of explanation text

Phase 1 outcome
To know what a good explanation looks and sounds like

PHASE 2

- Re-read extracts of the novel that explain how to care for Malkin; ask children to make notes
- Discuss their notes and add new ideas – what else might a mechanical pet need?
- Introduce new technical vocabulary and play talk games for children to orally rehearse
- Use text chunked in phase 1 to help plan it
- Provide opportunities for children to share and orally rehearse their ideas
- Finalise plans

Phase 2 outcome
To have planned my explanation

PHASE 3

- Shared write introductory paragraph – model how to use plan
- Children independently write the introduction
- Mark and follow-up on issues before they move onto the main body of the explanation
- Shared write to support with main body and concluding paragraphs
- Children independently write rest of explanation
- Support them to edit and refine whole text
- Add additional aspects such as diagrams
- Publish, share and evaluate

UNIT PLAN

Theme: *Cogheart* – Narrative Key Stage 2

FINAL OUTCOME:
To write a scary story for a Penny dreadful magazine

PHASE 1

- Re-read an extract of *Cogheart* that makes reference to the Penny dreadful (Lily and Anna)
- Research and present information to children about Penny dreadfuls (or Penny bloods), then explain the task
- Shared read a range of short spooky stories and respond (likes, dislikes, puzzles, patterns)
- Collect language & vocabulary that are effective
- Collect writer's hints — tricks that make an effective spooky story
- Use a map or storyboard to identify a typical spooky story plot

Phase 1 outcome
To know what a good spooky story looks and sounds like

PHASE 2

- Hook – Select an image of a ghostly pirate or highwayman and ask the children to generate ideas for a story based around the image
- Share ideas and support the children to begin to plan their stories
- Use drama and role-play to guide thinking through the main events
- Support the children to plan the story opening and ending
- Use oral rehearsal and further drama activities to check that the story planned is going to have the desired impact on the audience
- Support children to plan how they will incorporate vocabulary, language and suspense devices from phase 1
- Finalise plans

Phase 2 outcome
To have planned my story

PHASE 3

- Show children mock-up of Penny dreadful magazine
- Shared write opening to get the writing process started
- Children independently write the opening and next two paragraphs
- Mark and follow-up on issues before they move onto the next parts
- Shared write /children independently write next parts
- Mark and follow-up on issues before they move onto story ending
- Shared write /children independently write endings
- Support them to edit and refine story
- Publish in the Penny dreadful magazine, share and evaluate

UNIT PLANS

The Donkey Cabbage
Retold by Philip Pullman
(From Grimm Tales for Young and Old)

Persuasion
Adverts for: Donkey cabbages; wishing cloaks; Mount Garnet; travelling by cloud; one-sided arguments: kindness is king; giants should be avoided; storybook old women are trouble

Instructions
How to: use a donkey cabbage; use a wishing cloak; travel by cloud; avoid giants; trick a witch

Narrative
Change the characters and the setting; change the donkey; Wishing cloak story; giants story; story set on Mount Garnet

Information
Wishing cloaks; Mount Garnet; storybook witches; donkeys; cabbages; magic vegetables; cloud travel

UNIT PLAN

Theme: *The Donkey Cabbage* – Instructions

Key Stage 2

FINAL OUTCOME
Write a set of instructions for how to travel by cloud

PHASE 1

- Re-read part of *The Donkey Cabbage* when the hunter travels by cloud
- Explain task – to write a set of instructions for how to travel by cloud
- Shared read fantasy based sets of instructions, e.g. how to train a dragon, how to find a Gruffalo
- Explore and respond – compare & contrast
- Collect new effective vocabulary
- Identify the features and typical language of instructions
- Build list of writer's hints for fantasy based instructions
- Check children understand the typical chunks of instructions (introduction, what you need, what you do, conclusion)

Phase 1 outcome:
To know what a good set of Instructions looks and sounds like

PHASE 2

- Discuss who the audience might be for the how to travel by cloud instructions
- Using the extract from the story as a starting point, support children to develop ideas around the ordered steps for how to travel by cloud
- Use chunked set of instructions as basis for plan
- Use talk activities to support with ideas for adding detail into each step, e.g. Once you have reached the peak of the mountain, look out for low flying storm clouds
- Plan the steps
- Provide opportunities to support with planning the 'what you need' section followed by the 'introduction'
- Support with ideas for a concluding statement
- Finalise plan

Phase 2 outcome:
To have planned my instructions

PHASE 3

- Remind children of the audience for these instructions
- Shared write introduction
- Children write introduction and 'what you need' independently
- Shared write initial steps
- Children write steps independently
- Mark, feedback and follow-up on issues before moving on
- Shared write concluding statement
- Children complete independently
- Mark, feedback and edit
- Publish, share and evaluate

UNIT PLAN

Theme: *The Donkey Cabbage* – Narrative Key Stage 2

FINAL OUTCOME
Write a wishing cloak story

PHASE 1

- Re-read extracts from *The Donkey Cabbage* that mention the wishing cloak
- Ask children to imagine what the cloak looks like and then draw an outline of it
- Generate ideas about what else the wishing cloak could do – children write their ideas into the drawing
- Shared read and discuss other stories that they know that involve wishes, e.g. Aladdin, Magic Porridge Pot, *Squash and a Squeeze*
- Collect hints — what makes a good wishing story?
- Bank effective vocabulary and language
- Map the plot of a simple wishing story so that children understand structure

Phase 1 outcome:
To know what a good wishing story sounds like

PHASE 2

- Generate a plan using the map created in phase 1 for structure
- Begin by supporting the children to explore the characters in their story and the wishing cloak: Who are the main characters? Who has the cloak? Who gave it to them? Why?
- Provide drama and role-play opportunities for children to explore the plot to their story: What will the main events be? How will they start their stories? How will they end?
- Orally rehearse main ideas and keep adding to plans
- Finalise plans

Phase 2 outcome
To have planned my story

PHASE 3

- Brief shared write to get children started
- Children independently write the first paragraphs
- Mark and follow-up on issues before they move onto the other parts
- Shared write to support, where necessary
- Children independently write rest of the story
- Support them to edit and refine the story
- Publish, share and evaluate

USING NOVELS AND SHORT STORIES AS HOOKS

UNIT PLAN

Theme: *The Donkey Cabbage* – Persuasion

Key Stage 2

FINAL OUTCOME
Magazine and TV adverts for Donkey Cabbages

PHASE 1

- Hook – set up an Apprentice style task for the children to come up with an advertising campaign for Donkey Cabbages
- Watch TV adverts around a theme, e.g. toys, cars
- Shared read and discuss magazine adverts
- General discussion re adverts – Purpose? Audience? Tone? Which work best and why?
- Collect effective vocabulary and language structures (This will differ according to TV or written adverts)
- Generate writer's hints for TV adverts
- Generate writer's hints for magazine adverts

Phase 1 outcome
I know what persuasion is and what a good advertisement looks and sounds like

PHASE 2

- Identify the target audience for Donkey Cabbages adverts and agree the appropriate tone
- Using *The Donkey Cabbages* text, support the children to identify the attraction of Donkey Cabbages
- Support children to storyboard their TV adverts and then orally rehearse them (partners to evaluate and offer suggestions for editing)
- Now support children to plan their magazine adverts using the writer's hints collected in phase 1
- Orally rehearse and finalise ideas

Phase 2 outcome
I have planned my two adverts

PHASE 3

- Provide time for the children to record their TV adverts
- Share and evaluate
- Shared write a magazine advert
- Children independently write their magazine adverts
- Share, evaluate and re-draft
- Publish magazine adverts
- Present both adverts in the style of The Apprentice

Fireweed by Jill Paton Walsh

Persuasion
Letters: from Bill to his aunt asking her to pay for school; from Bill to Julie (end of Chapter 8); from Julie to her mum (Chapter 6); posters: staying safe; evacuation; rationing; sunlight soap van

Recount
Letters: from Bill's father; to Mrs Williams from Bill (Chapter 9); from Julie to her mum; Diaries: Dickie; Bill's father

Narrative
Short story in the first person by Julie; Dickie's story; Marco's story; short sequel; short prequel; Bill's father's story

Description
Places: bombed out homes and streets; war time London by day and by night; aunt's house before and after; sleeping inside an Anderson shelter or underground station; people: Pen portraits of Bill and Julie (before and during the war); Warden; fire watcher; Marco

UNIT PLAN

Theme: *Fireweed* – Setting Descriptions Key Stage 2

FINAL OUTCOME
Write two setting descriptions (War time London by day and by night)

PHASE 1

- Shared read variety of good quality setting descriptions (including extracts from Fireweed)
- Immerse children in setting descriptions so that they know the language structures by heart
- Collect writer's hints
- Explore the use of expanded noun phrases; metaphors, onomatopoeia, alliteration to add detail and effect
- Collect vocabulary and language
- Chunk a setting description into parts so that children understand structure
- Hook – read a description from *Fireweed*. Read it again and ask the children to sketch the scene whilst you read
- Discuss sketches drawing out how Jill Paton-Walsh uses language to enable the reader to picture the scene

Phase 1 outcome
To know what a good setting description sounds like

PHASE 2

- Explain task
- For each setting study extracts from *Fireweed* and build a vocabulary bank
- Play word/language games to continue to develop ideas, including use of the senses; expand the banked vocabulary with metaphors, onomatopoeia and alliteration
- Support the children to create a plan for each setting description
- Support children to 'talk' their descriptions to orally rehearse and refine them
- Finalise plans

Phase 2 outcome
To have planned my setting descriptions

PHASE 3

- For one of the settings: Model write first couple of lines (including modelling how to work from a plan)
- Children independently write their descriptions
- Mark, feedback and support them to edit and refine their writing
- Children independently write the second descriptions (putting into practice what they have learned from first setting descriptions)
- Edit, refine and publish
- Share both and evaluate

UNIT PLAN

Theme: *Fireweed* – Narrative Key Stage 2

FINAL OUTCOME
Short story written in the first person

PHASE 1

- Hook – re-read extracts from Chapter 1 of *Fireweed* in which Bill meets Julie
- Discuss Julie – what do we know about her? Where did she come from?
- Explain that the task is to innovate the opening of *Fireweed* by writing it from Julie's point of view
- Shared read extracts from *Fireweed* exploring the effect of writing in the first person
- Collect writer's hints for writing a first person narrative
- Construct a storyboard or map of the key events of Chapter 1 in order to help the children to structure their narratives

Phase 1 outcome
To know what makes a good first person narrative

PHASE 2

- Generate a plan using the ideas gathered in phase 1 for structure
- Provide drama and role-play opportunities for children to explore what might have happened to Julie and how she might have told her side of the story
- How will they start their stories? How will they end?
- Orally rehearse main ideas and keep adding to plans
- Check plans against writer's hints and amend
- Finalise plans

Phase 2 outcome
To have planned my story

PHASE 3

- Brief shared write to get children started
- Children independently write the first paragraphs
- Mark and follow-up on issues before they move onto the other parts
- Shared write to support, where necessary
- Children independently write rest of the story
- Support them to edit and refine the story
- Publish, share and evaluate

UNIT PLAN

Theme: *Fireweed* – Recount (Letter) Key Stage 2

FINAL OUTCOME
Write the letter from Julie to her mum telling her she's alive

PHASE 1
- Shared read letters, e.g. from My War Diary by Marcia Williams
- Compare & contrast; explore & respond – likes, dislikes, puzzles, patterns; and identify purpose of each, e.g. logging major events
- Collect effective vocabulary and language that portray feelings
- Use drama to bring letters alive; how would they be read? Received?
- Build a list of writer's hints for letters
- Explain the task

Phase 1 outcome
To know what a good war time letter sounds like

PHASE 2
- Support the children to develop ideas about what Julie's letter would say
- Explore how the children think a letter of this type would be structured and establish chunks for planning
- Orally rehearse ideas and begin to build plan
- Evaluate how well ideas portray feelings; add to plan
- Support children to plan each part of their letters
- Check plans against writer's hints and amend plans
- Finalise plans

Phase 2 outcome
To have planned my letter

PHASE 3
- Short shared write to get children's letters started
- Children write independently
- Mark and feedback; children edit and refine
- Read each other's letters and evaluate

176 UNIT PLANS

Grandpa's Story by Shaun Tan (From Tales from Outer Suburbia)

Persuasion
Scavenger hunt advert; visitor guide or brochure

Recount
Grandma's journal of her wedding day; wedding day recounts; postcards; social media status updates

Narrative
Tell the missing part of the story; write Grandma's version of the story; create a new Grandpa's story from the other side of the hill; create new stories using the settings

Information
Write the clues to the objects; survival guide to the places visited; unusual marriage traditions; rings and their symbolism; scavenger hunts

UNIT PLAN

Theme: *Grandpa's Story* – Narrative

Key Stage 2

FINAL OUTCOME
To write Grandma's Story (change viewpoint)

PHASE 1

- Read *Grandpa's Story*, respond and discuss it
- Work through the story and illustrations and map the main events (and places visited)
- Generate ideas about what might have happened at each of the places that are not described and bank the ideas
- Collect language & vocabulary that are effective
- Discuss what Shaun Tan has done to make this a good story and create a list of writer's hints

Phase 1 outcome
To know Grandpa's Story and what makes it a good story

PHASE 2

- Discuss the character of grandma – what do we know about her? What do we imagine her to be like? What would her version of the story be like?
- Explain task
- Using the map created in phase 1 as a guide, use talk activities and drama to imagine grandma's version the story
- Begin to plan ideas
- Orally rehearse main events using vocabulary and language collected at phase 1
- Support children to plan how they will incorporate elements of the writer's hints
- Finalise plan

Phase 2 outcome
To have planned my story

PHASE 3

- Shared write opening to get the writing process started
- Children independently write the opening
- Mark and follow-up on issues before they move onto the main paragraphs
- Shared write /children independently write main paragraphs
- Mark and follow-up on issues before they move onto the endings
- Children independently write endings
- Support them to edit and refine stories
- Publish, share and evaluate

UNIT PLAN

Theme: *Grandpa's Story* – Persuasion   **Key Stage 2**

FINAL OUTCOME
To write a travel brochure for the 'places' featured in *Grandpa's story*

PHASE 1

- Hook – discuss the places illustrated in *Grandpa's Story*; what do you imagine them to be like? Why has Shaun Tan drawn them in this way?
- Explain task. Discuss who might be interested in selling a holiday of this type and who might be the audience for such a brochure
- Shared read extracts from travel brochures
- Discuss purpose and how the writer tries to achieve this, and who the intended audience is and how the tone and form reflect this
- Collect writer's hints for a travel brochure text
- Collect and bank new vocabulary and language
- Chunk a typical travel brochure page to get a feel for structure

Phase 1 outcome
To know what a good travel brochure entry looks and sounds like

PHASE 2

- Using the illustrations from *Grandpa's Story*, support children to plan ideas
- Shape their ideas into plans using chunks from phase 1
- Play word and language games to support with the use of persuasive language
- Orally rehearse – support with development
- Finalise plans (bear in mind audience and purpose)

Phase 2 outcome
To have planned my travel brochure entries

PHASE 3

- Shared write a short persuasive piece to get the writing process started
- Children write their first one independently
- Mark, feedback and edit/refine
- Children write the rest of their brochure entries independently
- Mark, feedback and edit/refine
- Publish, share and evaluate

USING NOVELS AND SHORT STORIES AS HOOKS 179

UNIT PLAN	
Theme: *Grandpa's Story* – Recount	Key Stage 2

FINAL OUTCOME
To write grandpa's journal (or social media status updates)

PHASE 1
- Introduce task
- Discuss the purpose of a journal (or social media status update)
- Shared read journal entries and build a list of writer's hints for logs such as these
- Discuss how the entries are structured (if relevant)
- Collect vocabulary and language

Phase 1 outcome
To know what a short journal entry looks and sounds like

PHASE 2
- Map the main events of *Grandpa's story*
- Support the children to plan what they might say about each event if they were Grandpa
- Share ideas and refine
- Children complete a plan for their journal

Phase 2 outcome
To have planned my journal entries

PHASE 3
- Shared write a journal entry
- Children independently write their entries
- Mark and follow-up on issues throughout the writing process
- Support the children to edit and refine journal entries
- Publish, share and evaluate

Letters from the Lighthouse by Emma Carroll

Description
Contrasting settings: train carriage/seaside evening; city/seaside; lighthouse inside/outside; attic bedroom at Queenie's; Queenie's cellar; Olive's early morning walk

Recount
Pathé news reel performance; news reports: London zoo animals evacuated; lighthouse news; diaries: Air raids; being evacuated; first night at the lighthouse; first-person accounts: refugees; Mrs RB; Monsieur Bonet

Narrative
Change a part of the story to third person; write the conversation in chapter 1 between Sukie and 'the man'; Esther's story; Sukie's story; write the dialogue between Queenie and Ephraim

Information
WWII Female codebreakers; Spies; Women's Royal Voluntary Service; Kindertransport; Royal Pioneer Corps; Refugees; Romani people; government information on evacuation

UNIT PLAN
Theme: *Letters from the Lighthouse* – Information   Key Stage 2

FINAL OUTCOME
Information text on female codebreakers in WWII

PHASE 1
- Shared read a variety of information texts, including ones related to interesting people and jobs
- Compare & contrast; explore & respond
- Identify purpose & audience of each and how the tone and form relate to the purpose and audience
- Chunk a text into sections to establish the structure of an information text
- Collect and build transferable language
- Collect writer's hints for what makes a good information text

Phase 1 outcome
I know what a good information text looks and sounds like

PHASE 2
- Introduce task – to write an information text about female codebreakers
- Ask the children what they know about WWII codebreakers; collect ideas
- Support them to research the topic using a variety of sources (film/internet etc.)
- Support children to develop a plan; orally rehearse/discuss content of each section (using aspects from writer's hints list to make sure that it's as effective as possible)
- Finalise plans

Phase 2 outcome
I have planned my information text

PHASE 3
- Shared write introductory paragraph
- Children independently write introductory paragraph
- Edit and refine
- In turn shared write, children independently write, edit and refine next sections
- Shared/Independently write conclusion
- Refine to check for impact on reader
- Evaluate

UNIT PLAN

Theme: *Letters from the Lighthouse* – Narrative　　　　　　　　　　Key Stage 2

FINAL OUTCOME
To write an event in the third person

PHASE 1

- Choose an event from *Letters from the Lighthouse* that stood out for the children and explain the task
- Shared read extracts written in the third person and compare to extracts written in the first person – what's the effect? What does the writer have to do that is different?
- Build a list of writer's hints for turning a first person story into one written in the third person
- Analyse and collect language and vocabulary from a story written in the third person
- Read the chosen extract and discuss how it might have been different written in the third person

Phase 1 outcome
To know the difference between stories written in the first and third person and what makes each effective

PHASE 2

- Plot the main ideas to support the children with structure and planning
- Use oral rehearsal to help children to check out their ideas
- Support them to refine their thinking and annotate plans
- Finalise plans

Phase 2 outcome
To have planned my story

PHASE 3

- Shared write opening to get the writing process started
- Children independently write the opening and next paragraphs
- Mark and follow-up on issues before they move onto the final parts
- Shared write /children independently write next parts
- Support them to edit and refine story
- Publish, share and evaluate

USING NOVELS AND SHORT STORIES AS HOOKS 183

UNIT PLAN

Theme: *Letters from the Lighthouse* – Recount   Key Stage 2

FINAL OUTCOME
Write Monsieur Bonet's account of dad's final hours

PHASE 1

- Shared read the account of dad's final hours (United We Are Stronger chapter)
- Explain task – the children will be writing in role as M. Bonet telling Sukie
- Watch and shared read similar accounts; respond and discuss
- Analyse tone and the use of language and punctuation to portray emotion
- Build a list of writer's hints for this type of account
- Re-read the account and plot the events

Phase 1 outcome
To know what a good recount sounds like

PHASE 2

- Use drama to explore what M.Bonet might say about each and how he might say it (including his body language)
- Orally rehearse ideas and plan
- Check plans against writer's hints and amend
- Finalise plans

Phase 2 outcome
To have planned my recount

PHASE 3

- Short shared write to get children's recounts started
- Children write independently
- Mark and feedback; children edit and refine
- Read each other's recounts and evaluate

UNIT PLANS

Mackerel and Chips by Michael Morpurgo (From The Story Shop Compiled by Nikki Gamble)

Persuasion
Travel brochure pages: seaside holidays; Isles of Scilly; sea life environmental campaign leaflet; sea safety guide; First World War Dunkirk boat rescue request letter

Recount
Diaries/letters written by: Leah; the soldier; Mr Pender; Lifeboat crew member's diary; news report on Mr Pender's rescue

Narrative
New sea adventure for Leah; new sea rescue story; new story set by the sea; holiday themed story; Flashback stories: soldier's story; Leah telling it as an adult

Information
Sea rescue; lifeboats; boats; Isles of Scilly; seals; puffins; sea life; sea fish; fishing; Dunkirk evacuation

USING NOVELS AND SHORT STORIES AS HOOKS 185

UNIT PLAN

Theme: *Mackerel and Chips* – Information | Key Stage 2

FINAL OUTCOME
Magazine article on lifeboats

PHASE 1

- Shared read a variety of magazine style information texts (ideally about topics similar to this theme)
- Compare & contrast; explore & respond – likes, dislikes, puzzles, patterns; and identify purpose & audience of each
- Collect writer's hints for magazine articles
- Collect effective language and vocabulary
- Chunk a magazine article into sections to analyse structure
- Hook – re-cap the Mackerel and Chips story focussing on the rescue; watch a film clip about lifeboat rescues
- Explain task

Phase 1 outcome
I know what a good magazine information text looks and sounds like

PHASE 2

- Discuss who the audience might be for this writing, and decide on the appropriate form and tone
- Use texts read in Phase 1 to support children to consider what they could write about lifeboats (recommend sections on rescues as well as about the boats)
- Use chunks from phase 1 to start to plan the text
- Use talk activities to support with the development, and oral rehearsal, of ideas for each section of the plan
- Finalise plan
- Consider design aspects, if appropriate

Phase 2 outcome
I have planned my magazine article

PHASE 3

- Shared write opening section
- Children independently write opening section
- Mark, feedback and support children to edit, refine and evaluate
- Shared write other sections, where necessary
- Children independently write other sections
- Edit and refine to check for impact on reader
- Add design elements, if necessary
- Publish, share and evaluate

UNIT PLAN

Theme: *Mackerel and Chips* – Narrative   Key Stage 2

FINAL OUTCOME
To write an adventure story in a holiday setting

PHASE 1

- Hook – discuss where your children have been on holiday, e.g. caravan, hotel, staying with family etc. and ask what adventures they have had whilst there
- Read Mackerel and Chips and respond
- Chunk the basic plot into sections so that children understand how it is structured
- Collect and build upon language & vocabulary that are effective
- Shared read other stories in holiday settings
- Collect list of writer's hints for this type of story

Phase 1 outcome
To know what a good holiday adventure story looks and sounds like

PHASE 2

- Explain task
- Use drama to explore ideas for a new story
- Use the plot structure identified in phase 1 to begin to plan ideas
- Use oral rehearsal and further drama activities to develop ideas around the key events
- Plan main events, ending and opening
- Support children to plan how they will incorporate elements on the writer's hints list
- Finalise plan

Phase 2 outcome
To have planned my story

PHASE 3

- Shared write opening to get the writing process started
- Children independently write the opening and next paragraphs
- Mark and follow-up on issues before they move onto the final parts
- Shared write to support, where necessary
- Children independently write rest of the story
- Support them to edit and refine the story
- Share and evaluate

USING NOVELS AND SHORT STORIES AS HOOKS 187

UNIT PLAN

Theme: *Mackerel and Chips* – Persuasion | Key Stage 2

FINAL OUTCOME
Sea life campaign leaflet

PHASE 1

- Following reading *Mackerel and Chips* show the children a short film or photographs of sea pollution
- Discuss their responses and establish what they know about the subject and how they feel
- Explain that if you feel strongly about an issue you can campaign. Discuss different campaign methods, including leafletting the public
- Shared read a range of campaign leaflets
- Immerse the children in campaign leaflets so that they know some of the typical language structures
- Discuss design and layout and how these contribute to effect
- Collect and build on effective 'campaign' vocabulary and language
- Compile a list of writer's hints for campaign leaflets

Phase 1 outcome
I know what a good campaign leaflet looks and sounds like

PHASE 2

- Ensure that the topic is researched and that the children select an area that they feel is important to them
- Use drama/role-play to explore the arguments that you might put to the public as to why sea life is vital to preserve
- Support children to group their ideas into themes and generate persuasive sentences – orally rehearse to check that they sound right and have the right effect
- Check children are clear about purpose & audience for the leaflets
- Begin to plan leaflet
- Practise using elements of writer's hints as part of the arguments
- Orally rehearse each section of the leaflet; check tone; add vocabulary to plan
- Discuss layout decisions and finalise plan

Phase 2 outcome
I have planned my leaflet

PHASE 3

- Shared write opening of leaflet – model how to use plan
- Children independently draft the opening
- Mark and follow-up on issues before they move onto the main parts
- Shared write to support with main parts and closing
- Children independently draft rest of leaflet
- Support them to edit and refine whole text
- Publish polished text together with other design elements
- Share and evaluate

Discussion
Were teachers better in the old days? Were children better behaved in the old days? Were parents stricter in the old days? Were The Balaclava Boys trouble makers?

Description
Use real life experience to describe known characters and familiar settings; describe the main characters in detail; describe feelings

The Balaclava Story by George Layton
(From The Fib and Other Stories)

Narrative
Innovate the story with new characters, setting, item; write a modern version; short story with dialogue used to convey character; school based story

Information
Character profiles; schools past and present; school newsletter from the 1950s; George Layton's short stories study

USING NOVELS AND SHORT STORIES AS HOOKS

UNIT PLAN

Theme: *The Balaclava Story* – Discussion   Key Stage 2

FINAL OUTCOME
To write a discussion – Were parents stricter in the old days?

PHASE 1
- Read a range of discussion texts
- Explore purpose and audience for each; agree basic principles of these kinds of discussions
- Use talk activities to further explore the concept of 'discussion'
- Collect list of writer's hints
- Collect discursive language
- Play language games to practise using discursive language
- Chunk a discursive text into sections to clarify structure of discussion texts (Introduction, points for, points against, conclusion)

Phase 1 outcome
To know what good discussion texts look and sound like

PHASE 2
- Hook – explain the task then carry out a short discussion on the topic followed by a class vote
- Carry out a hot seating exercise in which the children hot seat an adult about parent strictness
- Ask the children to collect anecdotes from adults at home about their childhood experiences
- Support children to discuss arguments for and against, bringing in the anecdotes and hot seating work as evidence, and collate ideas
- Use chunks from phase 1 to start to plan new discussion
- Use language games to further explore the effective use of discursive language and weave this through the arguments already established
- Support children to plan introduction and conclusion
- Complete plan

Phase 2 outcome
To have planned my discussion text

PHASE 3
- Shared write introduction and points for paragraph/s
- Children independently write introduction and points for paragraph/s
- Mark and follow-up on issues before they move on
- Shared write points against and concluding paragraphs
- Children independently write points against and concluding paragraphs
- Mark and follow-up on issues
- Support with editing and refining discussions
- Share and evaluate
- Carry out a class vote, compare to original result!

UNIT PLAN

Theme: *The Balaclava Story* – Information Key Stage 2

FINAL OUTCOME
Information text comparing schools past and present

PHASE 1

- Shared read a variety of information texts (ideally about topics similar to this theme, such as toys past and present)
- Compare & contrast; explore & respond – likes, dislikes, puzzles, patterns; and identify purpose & audience of each
- Collect writer's hints for information texts
- Collect effective language and vocabulary
- Chunk an information page into sections to analyse structure
- Hook – Read extracts from *The Balaclava Story* that exemplify how schools were different in the 1950s and discuss
- Explain task

Phase 1 outcome
I know what a good information text looks and sounds like

PHASE 2

- Discuss who the audience might be for this writing, and decide on the appropriate form and tone
- Use texts read in Phase 1 to support children to consider what they could write about schools past and present
- Use chunks from phase 1 to start to plan the text (will they write two separate texts or one whole that compares aspects of schools past and present?)
- Use talk activities to support with the development, and oral rehearsal, of ideas for each section of the plan
- Finalise plan
- Consider design aspects, if appropriate

Phase 2 outcome
I have planned my information text

PHASE 3

- Shared write opening section
- Children independently write opening section
- Mark, and support children to edit, refine and evaluate
- Shared write other sections, where necessary
- Children independently write other sections
- Edit and refine to check for impact on reader
- Add design elements, if necessary
- Publish, share and evaluate

UNIT PLAN

Theme: *The Balaclava Story* – Narrative Key Stage 2

FINAL OUTCOME
Write a short narrative with dialogue to convey character

PHASE 1

- Re-read parts of *The Balaclava Story* where dialogue conveys character (e.g. dialogue between him and mum)
- Discuss how the dialogue, and description around it, conveys character
- Shared read and discuss other extracts of dialogue that convey character (e.g. from The Fib by G.Layton and Charlie & the Chocolate Factory by R.Dahl)
- Collect hints – how do writers use dialogue to convey character?
- Collect and bank effective language
- Explain task

Phase 1 outcome
To know how writers use dialogue to effectively convey character

PHASE 2

- Hook – use pictures of two characters talking, arguing etc. and generate ideas about what they might be saying etc.
- Now build up ideas about their personalities
- Bank ideas and generate vocabulary to support with conveying character (body language etc.)
- Support children to each choose and plan their short narrative involving these two characters
- Use drama and role-play to orally rehearse in pairs
- Children perform and evaluate their final ideas
- Finalise plans

Phase 2 outcome
To have planned my short narrative

PHASE 3

- Brief shared write to get children started
- Children independently write their short narratives
- Mark, feedback and support them to edit and refine their writing
- Publish, share and evaluate

The Girl of Ink and Stars by Kiran Millwood Hargrave

Persuasion
Trip Advisor: Isle of Joya, Crystal caves, Black Forests, Forgotten Territories, Governor Adori's Mansion; letters between Isabella and Lupe; Wanted posters: Lupe missing, search party members needed

Recount
Life in the Dedalo; news reports: Governor's Ship Burns; Governor's daughter lost; Adori's let-

Narrative
New ending to Arinta story; the story of how Da became a cartographer; a fire demon story; the legend of Grandfather Riosse's boat; Adori's story; quest set in Dedalo

Information
Cartography; astronomy; About: Yote the fire demon; Black forests; Tibicenas; Crystal caves; Dragon Fruit; The Forgotten Territories

USING NOVELS AND SHORT STORIES AS HOOKS 193

UNIT PLAN

Theme: *The Girl of Ink and Stars* – Narrative Key Stage 2

FINAL OUTCOME
To write a quest story set in Dedalo (labyrinth)

PHASE 1
- Explain the task
- Explore what children already know about quests and quest stories
- Begin to collect common themes and character types
- Shared read a range of quest stories and respond
- Collect language & vocabulary that are effective
- Collect list of writer's hints for a good quest story
- Use a map or mountain to plot the structure of a typical quest story

Phase 1 outcome
To know what a good quest story looks and sounds like

PHASE 2
- Re-read extracts from the novel to understand the setting (Dedalo) and how this will come into the children's quest stories; collect ideas
- Use the plot structure identified in phase 1 to begin to plan ideas; start with the story opening
- Discuss ideas and add to plan
- Discuss, orally rehearse and plan each part of the quest, incorporating effective vocabulary and language collected in phase 1
- Orally rehearse ideas and plan story ending
- Support children to plan how they will incorporate elements on the writer's hints list
- Finalise plan

Phase 2 outcome
To have planned my quest story

PHASE 3
- Shared write opening to get the writing process started
- Children independently write the opening and next two paragraphs
- Mark and follow-up on issues before they move onto the next parts
- Shared write /children independently write next parts
- Mark and follow-up on issues before they move onto story ending
- Shared write /children independently write endings
- Support them to edit and refine story
- Publish, share and evaluate

UNIT PLAN

Theme: *The Girl of Ink and Stars* – Persuasion **Key Stage 2**

FINAL OUTCOME
To write persuasive information and reviews about Governor Adori's mansion (in the style of Trip Advisor)

PHASE 1

- Re-read extracts about Governor Adori's mansion, including the Dedalo, from *The Girl of Ink and Stars* and discuss the setting: Assuming that the family no longer live there, do you think it would be a good place to stay? Why? Why not?
- Explain task. Discuss who might be interested in staying at Governor Adori's mansion and why (establish audience for information text)
- Choose a city or place and shared read some of the 'holiday rentals' on the Trip Advisor website
- Explore the overviews and amenity information provided
- Now read the reviews (you will need to vet these first!)
- Immerse the children in Trip Advisor style information
- Collect writer's hints for a Trip Advisor information piece
- Collect and bank new vocabulary and language
- Chunk a typical information page to get a feel for structure

Phase 1 outcome
To understand the Trip Advisor style of persuasive information and reviews

PHASE 2

- Using the extracts from the novel, support children to develop ideas for what they would include in their information page
- Begin to plan, using chunks from phase 1
- Play word and language games to support with the use of persuasive information
- Orally rehearse — support with development
- Finalise plan (bear in mind audience and purpose)
- Provide opportunities for children to consider what the reviews of the mansion might include

Phase 2 outcome
To have planned my persuasive information piece

PHASE 3

- Shared write a short persuasive information piece to get the writing process started
- Children write theirs independently
- Mark, feedback and edit/refine
- Shared write two or three short reviews
- Children write a few short reviews
- Mark, feedback and edit/refine
- Evaluate

UNIT PLAN

Theme: *The Girl of Ink & Stars* – News Report
Key Stage 2

FINAL OUTCOME
To write a news report – Governor's Ship Burns!

PHASE 1

- Hook – watch short news reels or read news articles about fire damaging buildings and places
- General discussion re news of this nature: audience, purpose, tone, form? How it is handled; sensationalism
- Shared read news reports in order to immerse the children in the language and tone
- Identify use of language and play language games to familiarise the children with it
- Plot the typical structure and check understanding (headline, 5 Ws intro para, story para, background/eye-witness para, concluding para)
- Collect writer's hints for a news report

Phase 1 outcome:
I know what a good news report sounds like

PHASE 2

- Re-read the extract that features Governor Adori's ship being burned
- Discuss the focus and key events that you could report on in a news report and explore through drama/freeze framing
- Hot seat characters and other parties to collect and develop ideas (including quotes)
- Support children to plan their reports
- Orally rehearse use of journalistic language; record key ideas
- Check plan against writer's hints, add to plan
- Finalise plan

Phase 2 outcome:
To have planned my news report

PHASE 3

- Shared write opening, incl. headline and use of language
- Independent & guided write openings
- Shared write next parts picking up on issues as report progresses
- Support with concluding paragraph—check it has impact
- Peer evaluate success, then edit
- Publish

The Grendel by Anthony Horowitz (From The Story Shop Compiled by Nikki Gamble)

Discussion
Should Beowulf be jailed for murder? Do two wrongs ever make a right? Is the Grendel story suitable for children?

Recount
News reports: Murder at Heoret; Heoret rises again; The Grendel is defeated; Investigation report; Beowulf's diary: crossing of a great sea; defeat of the Grendel

Narrative
Write the story of: Beowulf and the five giants; Beowulf and the sea serpents; prequel featuring the Grendel; tell the story from the viewpoint of a Geat

Description
King Hrothgar; Queen Wealtheow; Heoret; the Grendel; Beowulf; King Hygelac; the land of the Geats

USING NOVELS AND SHORT STORIES AS HOOKS 197

UNIT PLAN

Theme: *The Grendel* – Description & Action

Key Stage 2

FINAL OUTCOME
To write setting descriptions and action paragraphs in the style of Anthony Horowitz

PHASE 1

- Following reading and responding to *The Grendel*, focus on the action in the story
- Select a short section for children to learn by heart and perform (the purpose of this is to internalise the language)
- Use drama and role-play to bring the section to life and enable the children to understand it
- Bank the new vocabulary, explore meanings and collect synonyms
- Provide opportunities for children to generate sentences and paragraphs using the new vocabulary
- Share, discuss and evaluate in order to understand effective language use
- Repeat this process for setting descriptions

Phase 1 outcome
To know what good descriptions and action paragraphs sound like

PHASE 2

- Decide on theme for setting descriptions, e.g. another mythical place and share stimuli with children (photographs, film clips etc.)
- Generate and bank vocabulary
- Orally rehearse including bringing in vocabulary collected in phase 1
- Decide on theme for action paragraph, e.g. different mythical beast being fought and share stimuli with children (photographs, film clips etc.)
- Generate and bank vocabulary
- Orally rehearse including bringing in vocabulary collected in phase 1

Phase 2 outcome
To have orally rehearsed my description and action paragraphs

PHASE 3

Carry out the following process for both pieces of writing:
- Short shared write to get children started
- Children write independently
- Mark and feedback; children edit and refine
- Children read their writing aloud, selves and others evaluate

UNIT PLAN

Theme: *The Grendel* – Discussion　　　　　　　　　　　　　　Key Stage 2

FINAL OUTCOME
To write a discussion – Should Beowulf be jailed for murder?

PHASE 1

- Read a range of discussion texts
- Explore purpose and audience for each; agree basic principles of these kinds of discussions
- Use talk activities to further explore the concept of 'discussion'
- Collect list of writer's hints
- Collect discursive language
- Play language games to practise using discursive language
- Chunk a discursive text into sections to clarify structure of discussion texts (Introduction, points for, points against, conclusion)

Phase 1 outcome
To know what good discussion texts look and sound like

PHASE 2

- Hook – Explain the task then carry out a short discussion on the topic
- Use discursive drama techniques to explore arguments for and against and collate ideas
- Support the children to start planning using the chunks from phase 1
- Use language games to further explore the effective use of discursive language and weave this through the arguments already established
- Check plans against the list of writer's hints
- Refine and complete plan

Phase 2 outcome
To have planned my discussion text

PHASE 3

- Shared write introduction and points for paragraph/s
- Children independently write introduction and points for paragraph/s
- Mark and follow-up on issues before they move on
- Shared write points against and concluding paragraphs
- Children independently write points against and concluding paragraphs
- Mark and follow-up on issues
- Support with editing and refining discussions
- Share and evaluate

USING NOVELS AND SHORT STORIES AS HOOKS 199

UNIT PLAN	
Theme: *The Grendel* – Narrative	Key Stage 2

FINAL OUTCOME
To write a prequel about *The Grendel*

PHASE 1

- Read the opening of *The Grendel* and stop at '...it slithered through the mud and began to limp towards the hall.'
- Discuss *The Grendel* – what do we know about it? What do we think has happened to it previously?
- Shared read extracts from other stories that involve mythical beasts and collect plot ideas
- Collect language & vocabulary that are effective
- Use a map or story mountain to outline the basic plot of short story involving a mythical beast
- Collect list of writer's hints for beast stories

Phase 1 outcome
To know what a good 'beast' story looks and sounds like

PHASE 2

- Support children to think about a new story for *The Grendel* – Who will his enemy be? Why is he under attack? How is he beaten or how does he win the battle?
- Use drama to shape ideas into a story
- Begin to plan ideas
- Orally rehearse main events using vocabulary and language collected at phase 1
- Support children to plan how they will incorporate elements of the writer's hints
- Finalise plan

Phase 2 outcome
To have planned my *The Grendel* story

PHASE 3

- Shared write opening to get the writing process started
- Children independently write the opening and build up paragraphs
- Mark and follow-up on issues before they move onto the problem and resolution parts
- Shared write /children independently write problem, resolution and ending
- Support them to edit and refine story
- Publish, share and evaluate

The Legend of Podkin One-Ear by Kieran Larwood

Explanation
Brigid's How to…(spell) book; defence against the Gorm; guide to Life in Boneroot burrow; how a Gorm works; how to use a magical gift

Recount
Diary entries by main characters after key events; Lanica news articles; biographies of Hubert the Broad, Scramashank, Brigid

Narrative
Twelve gifts stories; Brigid's story (the witch in the woods); Crom's story; prequel (Sandywell warren and how the Gorm came to be)

Information
Bramblemas; Midwinter Rabbit; The Gorm; Gorm Rats & Birds; The bard; Realms of Lanica; Burrows, e.g. Thornwood, Munbury, Boneroot, Darkhollow; The Twelve Gifts; The witch in the woods

USING NOVELS AND SHORT STORIES AS HOOKS 201

UNIT PLAN
Theme: *The Legend of Podkin One-Ear* – Recount (Biography)   Key Stage 2

FINAL OUTCOME
To write a biography of Scramashank

PHASE 1

- Shared read short biographies, e.g. Marcia Williams' Three Cheers for Inventors
- Respond – likes, dislikes, puzzles, patterns; and identify purpose & audience
- General discussion re biographies: Check children understand the purpose and audience
- Immerse the children in short biographies
- Identify use of language, collect and create list of writer's hints
- Chunk a simple biography into sections (opening, childhood paragraph/s, later life paragraph/s, conclusion) so that children understand structure

Phase 1 outcome
I know what a good biography sounds like

PHASE 2

- Hook – re-read extracts from Podkin that describe Scramashank, e.g. at the end of Chapter 2
- Explain task
- Using clues from the novel, imagine how Scramashank became lord of The Gorm and his life before that at Sandywell
- Hot seat a Gorm expert to find out about his life
- Use chunks from phase 1 to plan biography
- Use talk activities to decide on extra detail, and orally rehearse ideas
- Orally rehearse use of effective language (collected in phase 1)
- Finalise plan

Phase 2 outcome
I have planned my biography

PHASE 3

- Shared write opening
- Independent & guided write openings
- Shared write next parts picking up on issues as biography progresses
- Support with concluding paragraph – check it has impact
- Check that the biography has a sensible chronological order and is interesting to read
- Edit and evaluate
- Publish

UNIT PLAN

Theme: *The Legend of Podkin One-Ear* – **Information**

Key Stage 2

FINAL OUTCOME
Wiki page on Bramblemas

PHASE 1

- Shared read a variety of information texts (ideally about topics such as *Christmas, Diwali, Chanukah,* celebrations)
- Compare & contrast; explore & respond – likes, dislikes, puzzles, patterns; and identify purpose & audience of each
- Collect writer's hints for information texts
- Study some Wiki pages and add to writer's hints (what makes a good Wiki page?)
- Collect effective language and vocabulary
- Chunk a Wiki page into sections to analyse structure, check understanding of purpose of each section

Phase 1 outcome
I know what a good information page looks and sounds like

PHASE 2

- Referring to the opening chapter of *The Legend of Podkin One-Ear*, explain the task
- Discuss who the audience might be for this writing
- Use texts read in phase 1 to support children to consider what they could write about Bramblemas
- Use chunks from phase 1 to start to plan the Wiki page
- Use talk activities to support with the development, and oral rehearsal, of ideas for each section of the plan
- Finalise plan
- Consider design aspects – how will they lay out their page? Will they add any photographs? Extra text?

Phase 2 outcome
I have planned my information page

PHASE 3

- Shared write opening section
- Children independently write opening section
- Mark, and support children to edit, refine and evaluate
- Shared write other sections, where necessary
- Children independently write other sections
- Edit and refine to check for impact on reader
- Add design elements
- Publish, share and evaluate

USING NOVELS AND SHORT STORIES AS HOOKS   203

UNIT PLAN

Theme: *The Legend of Podkin One-Ear* – **Narrative**   Key Stage 2

FINAL OUTCOME
Brigid's Story

PHASE 1

- Re-read parts of Chapter 7 The Witch in the Woods and discuss Brigid's character
- Bringing in clues from later chapters, create a pen-portrait of Brigid
- Explain task
- Use drama to explore ideas around Brigid's story – what's happened previously? How might her story end?
- Draw upon previous story maps or mountains to consider how her story might be structured
- Use previous learning to collect hints — what makes a good story?

Phase 1 outcome
To know Brigid's character and begin to consider what her story may be

PHASE 2

- Generate a plan using the map or mountain created in phase 1 for structure
- Provide drama and role-play opportunities for children to explore the plot to their story:
- Are they going to include Podkin characters? Where within Brigid's story?
- How will they start their stories? How will they end?
- Orally rehearse main ideas and keep adding to plans
- Finalise plans

Phase 2 outcome
To have planned my story

PHASE 3

- Brief shared write to get children started
- Children independently write the first paragraphs
- Mark and follow-up on issues before they move onto the other parts
- Shared write to support, where necessary
- Children independently write rest of story
- Support them to edit and refine story
- Publish, share and evaluate

The Tale of Despereaux by Kate DiCamillo

Discussion
Is Despereaux a hero; Does Furlough cares about Despereaux; Are rats more powerful than mice; Is the Princess a powerful character

Description
Characters: Despereaux, Gregory, Miggery Sow, Princess, Botticelli, Roscuro; Settings: Castle dungeons, kitchen, banquet hall

Narrative
Prequels: Mouse mother Antionette's story; Gregory the Jailer's story; new adventure for Princess and Despereaux; new story set in the castle

Instructions
How to be a mouse manual; how to be an effective mouse council; how to make soup; how to look after a pet mouse or rat

UNIT PLAN

Theme: *The Tale of Despereaux* – Discussion

Key Stage 2

FINAL OUTCOME
To write a discussion – Are rats more powerful than mice?

PHASE 1

- Read a range of discussion texts
- Explore purpose and audience for each; agree basic principles of these kinds of discussions
- Use talk activities to further explore the concept of 'discussion'
- Collect list of writer's hints
- Collect discursive language
- Play language games to practise using discursive language
- Chunk a discursive text into sections to clarify structure of discussion texts (Introduction, points for, points against, conclusion)

Phase 1 outcome
To know what good discussion texts look and sound like

PHASE 2

- Hook - explain the task then carry out a short discussion on the topic (based on evidence from The Tale of Despereaux) followed by a class vote
- Using evidence from the novel, support children to discuss arguments for and against and collate ideas
- Bring in other well-known stories with mouse/rat characters to add to ideas, e.g. The Gruffalo, Charlotte's Web, The Lion & the mouse fable
- Use chunks from phase 1 to start to plan new discussion
- Use language games to further explore the effective use of discursive language and weave this through the arguments already established
- Complete plan

Phase 2 outcome
To have planned my discussion text

PHASE 3

- Shared write introduction and points for paragraph/s
- Children independently write introduction and points for paragraph/s
- Mark and follow-up on issues before they move on
- Shared write points against and concluding paragraphs
- Children independently write points against and concluding paragraphs
- Mark and follow-up on issues
- Support with editing and refining discussions
- Share and evaluate
- Carry out a class vote, compare to original result!

UNIT PLAN

Theme: *The Tale of Despereaux* – Instructions   Key Stage 2

FINAL OUTCOME
Write the Tilling family instructions for how to be a mouse

PHASE 1
- Explain task – to write a set of instructions for how to be a mouse
- Re-read extracts from the opening chapters of *The Tale of Despereaux* asking children to take notes as if they have to instruct Despereaux on how to be a mouse
- Shared read less traditional sets of instructions, e.g. how to be a celebrity
- Explore and respond; compare & contrast
- Identify the features and typical language of these types of instructions (e.g. introduction, what you do, concluding statement)
- Collect writer's hints for instructions
- Chunk text into sections and discuss layout (refer to purpose and audience)

Phase 1 outcome
To know what a good set of Instructions looks and sounds like

PHASE 2
- Re-visit the notes children took from the opening chapters and add to them by reading other passages from the novel that explore how to be a mouse
- Using the 'what you do' section as a starting point for planning begin to orally rehearse and then plan each step
- Use talk activities to support with ideas for adding detail into each step
- Use talk activities to support with ideas for what you might put into an introduction and a conclusion
- Complete plan

Phase 2 outcome
To have planned my instructions

PHASE 3
- Shared write introduction and the start of the what you do section
- Children write introduction and start of what you do section independently
- Mark, feedback and follow-up on issues before moving on
- Picking up on issues, shared write next part
- Children write next part independently
- Mark, feedback and follow-up on issues before moving on
- Shared write concluding statement
- Children complete independently
- Mark, feedback and edit
- Publish, share and evaluate

USING NOVELS AND SHORT STORIES AS HOOKS

UNIT PLAN

Theme: *The Tale of Despereaux* – Narrative

Key Stage 2

FINAL OUTCOME
To write a story in a castle setting

PHASE 1

- Referring to *The Tale of Despereaux*, explain task
- Shared read short stories in a similar setting and collect themes, e.g. royal families, heroes, villains
- Select one story that grips the children and re-read
- Collect language & vocabulary that are effective
- Chunk the basic plot into sections so that children understand it
- Collect list of writer's hints for this type of story

Phase 1 outcome
To know what a good story set in a castle looks and sounds like (plot & language)

PHASE 2

- Use drama to explore ideas for a new story set in a castle
- Use the plot structure identified in phase 1 to begin to plan ideas
- Use oral rehearsal and further drama activities to develop ideas around the key events
- Plan main events, ending and opening
- Support children to plan how they will incorporate elements on the writer's hints list
- Finalise plan

Phase 2 outcome
To have planned my story

PHASE 3

- Shared write opening to get the writing process started
- Children independently write the opening and build up paragraphs
- Mark and follow-up on issues before they move onto the problem and resolution parts
- Shared write to support, where necessary
- Children independently write rest of story
- Support them to edit and refine story
- Share and evaluate

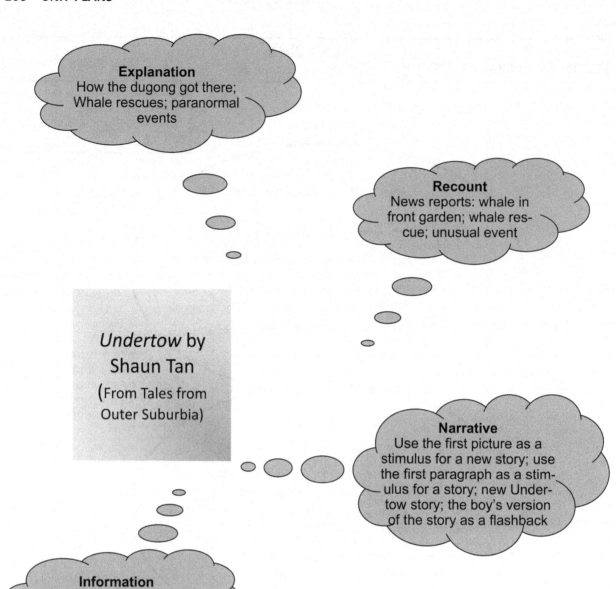

UNIT PLAN	
Theme: *Undertow* – Explanation	Key Stage 2

FINAL OUTCOME
Explanation of how the dugong got there

PHASE 1

- Shared read a variety of explanation texts (including events such as crop circles or alien sightings)
- Respond, identify audience and purpose of each and how the form and tone reflect the intended audience
- Collect effective vocabulary/language of these types of explanations
- Review any design aspects that are particularly useful for readers, e.g. diagrams
- Chunk an explanation text into parts so that children understand the structure – introduction, explanation of aspects (including eye witness/expert quotes), conclusion
- Create a list of writer's hints for explanation texts
- Explain task and discuss who the audience might be for such a text

Phase 1 outcome
To know what a good explanation looks and sounds like

PHASE 2

- Agree on the form and tone of the explanation text
- Use drama to begin to plan the contents of the explanation – where could it have come from? How could it have got there? Hot seat a dugong expert
- Support children to plan the main body of the explanation
- Provide opportunities for children to share and orally rehearse their ideas
- Support children to plan their introductory paragraph/s and conclusion
- Finalise plans

Phase 2 outcome
To have planned my explanation

PHASE 3

- Shared write introductory paragraph – model how to use plan
- Children independently write the introduction
- Mark and follow-up on issues before they move onto the main body of the explanation
- Shared write to support with main body
- Children independently write main body
- Mark and follow-up on issues before moving onto the concluding paragraph
- Shared/independent write conclusion
- Support them to edit and refine whole text
- Add additional aspects such as diagrams
- Publish, share and evaluate

UNIT PLAN

Theme: *Undertow* – Narrative

Key Stage 2

FINAL OUTCOME
Short story using the first paragraph of *Undertow* as a starter

PHASE 1

- Hook – re-read the first paragraph of *Undertow*, stopping at the colon before the final clause
- Provide opportunities for children to collaborate and consider what a new story might be about; bank ideas
- Take a few key ideas and facilitate the children to expand on them in order to generate more ideas – Where could each story be set? Who lives in the house at no.17? Will it be a big, unusual event?
- Study some maps or mountains of short stories in order to help the children to consider how their stories will be structured; ask them to choose a structure

Phase 1 outcome
To hook the children into coming up with a new short story

PHASE 2

- Support children to plan their new short story based on their chosen plot structure
- Provide drama and role-play opportunities for children to explore their plot ideas
- How will they start their stories? How will they end?
- Orally rehearse main ideas
- Finalise plans

Phase 2 outcome:
To have planned my story

PHASE 3

- Brief shared write to get children started
- Children independently write the first paragraphs
- Mark and follow-up on issues before they move onto the other parts
- Shared write to support, where necessary
- Children independently write rest of story
- Support them to edit and refine story
- Publish, share and evaluate

USING NOVELS AND SHORT STORIES AS HOOKS

UNIT PLAN

Theme: *Undertow* – News Report

Key Stage 2

FINAL OUTCOME
To write a news report – Live whale found in front garden!

PHASE 1

- Hook – watch short news reels or read news articles about unusual events
- General discussion re news of this nature: audience, purpose, tone, form? How it is handled; sensationalism
- Shared read news reports in order to immerse the children in the language and tone
- Identify use of language and play language games to familiarise the children with it
- Plot the typical structure and check understanding (headline, 5 Ws intro para, story para, background/eye-witness para, concluding para)
- Collect writer's hints for a news report

Phase 1 outcome
I know what a good news report sounds like

PHASE 2

- Share the illustration of the dugong in the front garden
- Discuss what you could report on in a news report and explore through drama
- Hot seat characters and other parties to collect and develop ideas (including quotes)
- Support children to plan their reports using chunks from phase 1
- Orally rehearse use of journalistic language; record key ideas
- Check plan against writer's hints, add to plan
- Finalise plan

Phase 2 outcome
To have planned my own news report

PHASE 3

- Shared write opening, incl. headline and use of language
- Independent & guided write openings
- Shared write next parts picking up on issues as report progresses
- Support with concluding paragraph – check it has impact
- Peer evaluate success, then edit
- Publish

UNIT PLANS

Varjak Paw by SF Said

Persuasion
One sided argument: Why Varjak should leave the Contessa's house; why Varjak should remain at the Contessa's house; Advertise the seven skills in the way of Jalal

Description
Characters: Elder Paw; Varjak; Julius; Holly; Sally Bones; Cudge; Jalal; Settings: Contessa's house (compare old & current); garden; wall; city; traffic; Mesopotomia

Narrative
Jalal Tale; Jalal's flashback to life in the Contessa's house; short suspense story in city setting; Black cat's story; another cat's adventure (for example, Holly, Ginger, Sally); re-write ending from Cudge's point of view

Information
Mosopotamian Blue Cats; Mesopotamia; the city; Street cats survival guide; biography of Holly; the way (martial arts for cats); vanishings

UNIT PLAN

Theme: *Varjak Paw* – Information   Key Stage 2

FINAL OUTCOME
Street Cats Survival Guide

PHASE 1

- Shared read a variety of information texts (ideally guides such as pet care, social media, gardening)
- Compare & contrast; explore & respond – likes, dislikes, puzzles, patterns; and identify purpose & audience of each
- Collect writer's hints for these types of information texts
- Collect effective language and vocabulary
- Chunk a guide into sections to analyse structure, check understanding of purpose of each section
- Hook – mock up a cover of the Street Cats Survival Guide, show the children and explain task

Phase 1 outcome
I know what a good 'guide' text looks and sounds like

PHASE 2

- Discuss who the audience might be for this writing; what might the tone be?
- Use texts read in Phase 1 to support children to consider what information they could include in a survival guide for street cats
- Use chunks from Phase 1 to start to plan the guide
- Use talk activities to support with the development, and oral rehearsal, of ideas for each section of the plan
- Finalise plan
- Consider design aspects – how will they lay out their guide? Will they add any photographs? Extra text?

Phase 2 outcome
I have planned my guide

PHASE 3

- Shared write opening section
- Children independently write opening section
- Mark, and support children to edit, refine and evaluate
- Shared write other sections, where necessary
- Children independently write other sections
- Edit and refine to check for impact on reader
- Add design elements
- Publish, share and evaluate

UNIT PLAN

Theme: *Varjak Paw* – Narrative

Key Stage 2

FINAL OUTCOME
Short story with suspense featuring Holly the cat

PHASE 1

- Hook – re-read extracts from *Varjak Paw* that tell us about Holly the cat
- Discuss her character and generate ideas for other stories Holly may have to tell
- Use drama to explore ideas (suggest that they are dark, fear stories)
- Explain task
- Shared read short stories with suspense and respond
- Collect effective language and vocabulary
- Collect writer's hints for what makes a good suspense story
- Draw upon previous story maps or mountains to consider how Holly's story might be structured (could be traditional 5 parts: opening, build up, problem, resolution, ending)

Phase 1 outcome
To know Holly's character and what makes a good story with suspense

PHASE 2

- Generate a plan using the ideas gathered in phase 1 for structure
- Provide drama and role-play opportunities for children to explore the plot to their story
- How will they start their stories? How will they end?
- Orally rehearse main ideas and keep adding to plans
- Support with how atmosphere will be created and how suspense will be used effectively
- Check plans against writer's hints and amend
- Finalise plans

Phase 2 outcome:
To have planned my story

PHASE 3

- Brief shared write to get children started
- Children independently write the first paragraphs
- Mark and follow-up on issues before they move onto the other parts
- Shared write to support, where necessary
- Children independently write rest of story
- Support them to edit and refine story
- Publish, share and evaluate

UNIT PLAN

Theme: *Varjak Paw* – Persuasion
Key Stage 2

FINAL OUTCOME
Write a one-sided argument – why Varjak should not leave the Contessa's house

PHASE 1

- Hook – re-read extracts from the start of the novel which are about how Varjak feels about his home
- Explain task: To write a one-sided argument about why Varjak should not leave the house (imagine a member of Varjak's family is writing it)
- Shared read one-sided argument texts
- Compare and contrast – which works best and why?
- Identify the tone of each and how this relates to audience
- Identify use of language, collect and check understanding of what makes it effective
- Collect list of writer's hints for one-sided arguments
- Chunk a one-sided argument text into sections to help children understand structure (introduction, 2/3 paragraphs each with a main point and explanation/justification, conclusion)

Phase 1 outcome
I know what a good one-sided argument text looks and sounds like

PHASE 2

- Use chunks from phase 1 to plan, start with main points
- Use drama/role-play to explore the arguments that you might for Varjak staying at home
- Group ideas into themes and generate persuasive sentences – orally rehearse to check that they sound right and have the right effect
- Generate ideas and plan introductions and conclusions
- Take elements from the list of hints and practise using them as part of the arguments
- Orally rehearse each section
- Add vocabublary to plan
- Check planned ideas are appropriate
- Finalise plan

Phase 2 outcome
I have planned my one-sided argument text

PHASE 3

- Shared write introduction
- Children independently write their introduction
- Mark and follow-up on issues before they move onto the main parts
- Shared write to support with main parts
- Children independently write main parts
- Mark and follow-up on issues before they move onto the conclusion
- Shared write conclusion
- Children independently write their conclusion
- Mark and follow-up on issues; support with editing and refining
- Share and evaluate

References

Books

Barrs, M. and Cork, V. (2001) *The Reader in the Writer*, London: Centre for Language in Primary Education.

Bearne, E. (2002) Multimodal narratives, in M. Barrs & S. Pidgeon (eds) *Boys and Writing* London: Centre for Literacy in Primary Education (p. 27).

Chambers, A. (1993) *Tell Me: Children Reading and Talk*, Gloucester: Thimble Press.

Corbett, P. (2008) *Talk for Writing in Practice: The Teaching Sequence for Writing*, 00467-2008PDF-EN-21, London: HMSO.

Dudley, P. (2011) *Lessons for Learning: How Teachers Learn in Contexts of Lesson Study*, Unpublished Doctoral Thesis, University of Cambridge (p. 208).

Fisher, R., Myhill, D., Jones, S. and Larkin, S. (2010) *Using Talk to Support Writing*, London: Sage.

Martin, A., Lovat, C. and Purnell, G. (2004) *The Really Useful Literacy Book: Being Creative with Literacy in the Primary Classroom*, 2nd edn, London: Routledge.

Ofsted (2011) *Excellence in English: What We Can Learn from 12 Outstanding Schools (100229)*, London: DfE.

Primary National Strategies (2008) *Talk for Writing*, London: DCSF

UKLA and PNS (2004) *Raising Boys' Achievements in Writing*.

Internet

Assessment Reform Group (2002) http://www.aaia.org.uk/category/afl/

Department for Education (2013) *The National Curriculum in England Key Stages 1 and 2 Framework Document* https://www.gov.uk/government/publications/national-curriculum-in-england-primary-curriculum

Parietti, K. (2013) http://www.theguardian.com/teacher-network/teacher-blog/2013/feb/01/teaching-creative-writing-ideas-activities-primary-literacy

Children's books

Ahmed and the Feather Girl by Jane Ray (2010) Frances Lincoln Children's Books
Amazing Grace by Mary Hoffman and Caroline Binch (1991) Frances Lincoln Books
Cogheart by Peter Bunzl (2016) Usborne Publishing Ltd.
Fireweed by Jill Paton Walsh (1969) Macmillan
Grimm Tales for Young and Old by Philip Pullman (2012) Penguin Classics
Journey by Aaron Becker (2013) Walker Books
King Arthur and the Knights of the Round Table Retold & Illustrated by Marcia Williams (1996) Walker Books
Letters from the Lighthouse by Emma Carroll (2017) Faber & Faber
Lion at School and Other Stories by Philippa Pearce (1986) Puffin Books
Mr Majeika by Humphrey Carpenter (1984) Puffin Books
Mrs Pepperpot Stories by Alf PrØysen (1959) Red Fox
My Secret War Diary by Marcia Williams (2008) Walker Books
Naughty Bus by Jan and Jerry Oke (2004) Little Knowall Publishing
One Snowy Night by Nick Butterworth (1989) Harper Collins Children's Books
Pandora by Victoria Turnbull (2016) Frances Lincoln Children's Books
Prokofiev's Peter and the Wolf Retold and Illustrated by Ian Beck (1995) Picture Corgi Books
Quest by Aaron Becker (2014) Walker Books
Stick Man by Julia Donaldson and Axel Scheffler (2008) Alison Green Books
Storm Whale by Sarah Brennan (2017) Old Barn Books Limited
Tad by Benji Davies (2019) Harper Collins Children's Books
Tales from Outer Suburbia by Shaun Tan (2008) Templar Books
The Dark by Lemony Snicket (2013) Orchard Books
The Day the Crayons Quit by Drew Daywalt and Oliver Jeffers (2013) Harper Collins Children's Books
The Disgusting Sandwich by Gareth Edwards and Hannah Shaw (2013) Alison Green Books
The Egg by M.P. Robertson (2000) Frances Lincoln Children's Books
The Elephant's Friend and Other Tales from Ancient India Retold by Marcia Williams (2012) Walker Books
The Enchanted Wood by Enid Blyton (1939) Newnes
The Fib and Other Stories by George Layton (2001) Pan Macmillan
The Girl of Ink and Stars by Kiran Millwood Hargrave (2016) Chicken House
The Ice Bear by Jackie Morris (2017) Graffeg Limited
The Legend of Podkin One-Ear by Kieran Larwood (2016) Faber & Faber
The Lighthouse Keeper's Lunch by Ronda and David Armitage (1977) Scholastic
The Story Shop (Stories for Literacy) Compiled by Nikki Gamble (2006) Hodder
The Story Tree (Tales to Read Aloud) Retold by Hugh Lupton (2001) Barefoot Books
The Tear Thief by Carol-Ann Duffy and Nicoletta Ceccoli (2007) Barefoot Books
The Tale of Despereaux by Kate DiCamillo (2004) Walker Books
The Tiger Who Came to Tea by Judith Kerr (1973) Picture Lions
The Tin Forest by Helen Ward and Wayne Anderson (2001) Templar Books
The True Story of the Three Little Pigs by Jon Scieszka (1991) Puffin Books
The Twits by Roald Dahl (1980) Puffin Books
The Way Back Home by Oliver Jeffers (2007) Harper Collins Children's Books
Three Cheers for Inventors! by Marcia Williams (2005) Walker Books
Varjak Paw by S. F. Said, illustrated by David McKean (2014) Penguin Random House Children's UK

Quick guide to completing a gaps sheet

1. Identify what your ideal final written outcome will be, for example, short story with accurately punctuated dialogue.

2. Use that to construct a short baseline writing task, for example, show a picture of two people deep in conversation or arguing and ask the children to write what they think the dialogue may be.

3. Read the baseline writings and establish the **main** issues that need tackling.

4. Prioritise the issues so that you have three: (1) words and language, (2) text structure, (3) sentence structure and punctuation.

5. Decide on what you are going to teach to help to develop these areas of learning (teaching objectives).

6. For each issue, decide on a child-friendly target (learning outcomes).

7. Establish how you are going to differentiate the targets according to need.

Writing Gaps Grid

Class: Date:

Assessment	Next steps
Key issues	**Key objectives**	**Key learning outcomes/targets** (I can..., I know..., I understand):
Words/Language	Words/Language	Words/Language
Text structure	Text structure	Text structure
Sentence construction & punctuation	Sentence construction & punctuation	Sentence construction & punctuation

This grid can be found here: www.literacyfocus.co.uk My Book tab

APPENDIX 221

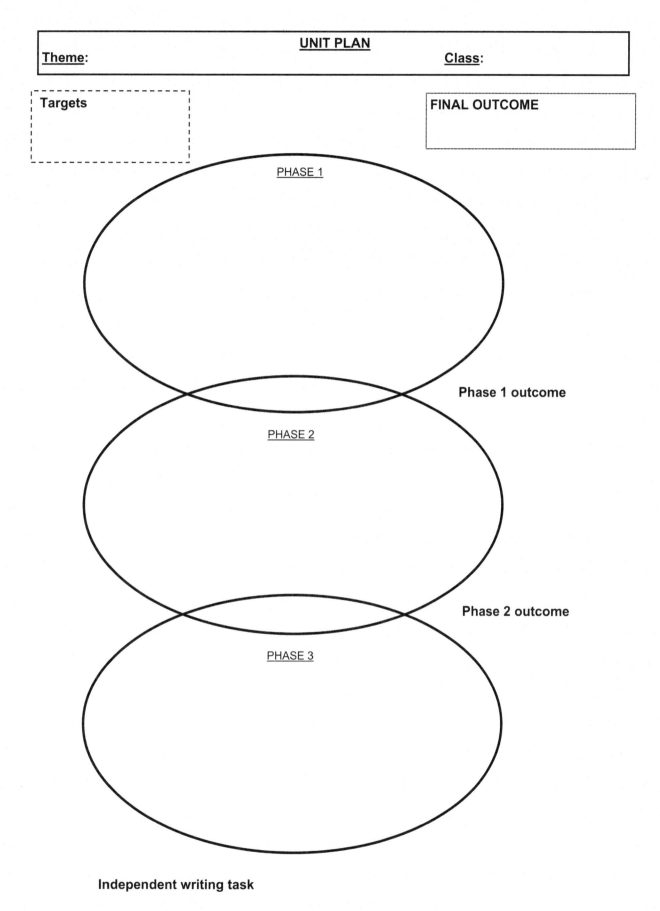

An editable version of this planner can be found here: www.literacyfocus.co.uk My Book tab

Circles planning: quick guide

Step 1: Decide on the text type that you want children to produce. Complete the Final Outcome box. For example, *write an information leaflet*.

Step 2: Complete the baseline assessment and generate targets.

Step 3: Use the targets to add to the final outcome. For example, *write an information leaflet with a clear structure and technical vocabulary*.

Step 4: Complete the outcome for phase 1. For example, *I know what a good information leaflet looks and sounds like*.

Step 5: Complete the outcome for phase 2. For example, *I know what information will go into my leaflet and I have planned it out*.

Step 6: List the activities that will be carried out during the three phases.

Step 7: Go through and slot in 'target' teaching.

Step 8: Go through and slot in short writing opportunities, if necessary.

Step 9: Plan the hook.

Consider:
- Audience and purpose for writing? Where will it be published?
- Independent writing task

PHASE 1
Immersion in text
Shared reading
Enjoy, explore, and respond to text
Develop comprehension skills
Identify language/genre features
Collect writer's hints and vocabulary

PHASE 2
Gather ideas
Oral rehearsal
Plan

PHASE 3
<u>Shared writing</u>
Teacher modelling
Teacher scribing
Supported composition
<u>Guided writing</u>
Independent writing
Draft, revise, edit

Index

Italicized pages refer to figures.

Ahmed and the Feather Girl (Ray) 66–69; instruction 67; narrative 68; news report 69
Amazing Grace (Hoffman) 16–19; information 16, 17; narrative 16, 18; persuasion 16, 19; recount 16
Anderson, W.: *Tin Forest, The* 102–105
Armitage, D.: *Lighthouse Keeper's Lunch, The* 48–51
Armitage, R.: *Lighthouse Keeper's Lunch, The* 48–51
assessment(s) xi; as cold writes xiii; formative xi; information gathering xiii–xiv; for learning xi; non-fiction xiii; record xiii; robust xiii; summative xi, xiii
Assessment Reform Group xi

Balaclava Story, The (Lyton) 188–191; discussion 189; information 190; narrative 191
Barrs, M. 8
baseline writing xiii
Bearne, E. 1
Becker, A.: *Journey* 20–23; *Quest* 74–77
Blue Coat, The (Lupton) 146–149; information 147; instructions 148; narrative 149
Blyton, E.: *Enchanted Wood, The* 150–153
booktalk 5
Brave Little Tailor, The (Pullman) 160–163; discussion 161; explanation 162; narrative 163
Brennan, S.: *Storm Whale* 82–85
Bunzl, P.: *Cogheart* 164–167
Butterworth, N.: *One Snowy Night* 28–31

Carpenter, H.: *Mr Majeika* 126–129
Carroll, E.: *Letters from the Lighthouse* 180–183
Ceccoli, N.: *Tear Thief, The* 52–55
Chambers, A. 5
chunk(s) 12
circles planning approach 1–10; elements 7–8; independent writing 2–7, 8–9; model texts 8; overview 1–2; process to complete 9–10; tools 8
class targets xiii–xiv
Cogheart (Bunzl) 164–167; description 165; explanation 166; narrative 167
combined knowledge *xii*
compare and contrast 11
Corbett, P. 6, xii
Cork, V. 8
curriculum xi; expectations xiii; teacher's knowledge of the pupils' learning and xi; writing 3, xiii

Dahl, R.: *Twits, The* 154–157
Dark, The (Snicket) 86–89; explanations 87; informations 88; narrative 89
Davies, B.: *Tad* 36–39
Day the Crayons Quit, The (Daywalt and Jeffers) 8, 40–43; narrative 41; persuasion 42; recount 43
Daywalt, D. 8; *Day the Crayons Quit, The* 40–43
descriptions: *Cogheart* (Bunzl) 165; *Fireweed* (Walsh) 173; *Grendel, The* (Horowitz) 197;

226 INDEX

Lighthouse Keeper's Lunch, The (Armitage and Armitage) 49; *Lion at School* (Pearce) 119; *Pandora* (Turnbull) 71; *Storm Whale* (Brennan) 83; *Tad* (Davies) 37; *Tear Thief, The* (Duffy and Ceccoli) 53

DiCamillo, K.: *Tale of Despereaux, The* 204–207
direct teaching 7–8
discussion: *Balaclava Story, The* (Layton) 189; *Brave Little Tailor, The* (Pullman) 161; *Grendel, The* (Horowitz) 198; *Sir Lancelot's First Quest* (Williams) 79; *Storm Whale* (Brennan) 84; *Tale of Despereaux, The* (DiCamillo) 205; *True Story of the 3 Little Pigs, The* (Scieszka) 107
Disgusting Sandwich, The (Edwards and Shaw) 44–47; instructions 45; narrative 46; recount 47
Donaldson, J.: *Stick Man* 32–35
Donkey Cabbage, The (Pullman) 168–171; instruction 169; narrative 170; persuasion 171
Duffy, C. A.: *Tear Thief, The* 52–55

Edwards, G.: *Disgusting Sandwich, The* 44–47
Egg, The (Robertson) 90–93; explanation 91; narrative 92; recount letter 93
Elephant's Friend, The (Williams) 94–97; information text 95; narrative 96; persuasion 97
Enchanted Wood, The (Blyton) 150–153; explanation 151; information 152; narrative 153
experimentation 6
explanations: *Brave Little Tailor, The* (Pullman) 162; *Cogheart* (Bunzl) 166; *Dark, The* (Snicket) 87; *Egg, The* (Robertson) 91; *Enchanted Wood, The* (Blyton) 151; *Journey* (Becker) 21; *Lighthouse Keeper's Lunch, The* (Armitage and Armitage) 50; *Lion at School* (Pearce) 120; *Mr Majeika* (Carpenter) 127; *Peter and the Wolf* (Prokofiev) 139; *Quest* (Becker) 75; *Tad* (Davies) 38; *Undertow* (Tan) 209
extended write/completion of text 6–7

Fireweed (Walsh) 172–175; description 173; narrative 174; recount 175
Fisher, R. 6
formative assessments xi

gaps teaching 7–8
generic writing skills xiii
Girl of Ink and Stars, The (Hargrave) 8, 192–195; narrative 193; news report 195; persuasion 194
Grandpa's Story (Tan) 176–179; narrative 177; persuasion 178; recount 179
Great Sharp Scissors (Pearce) 114–117; narrative 115; persuasion 116; recount 117
Grendel, The (Horowitz) 196–199; description and action 197; discussion 198; narrative 199
guided writing 7

Hargrave, K. M. 8; *Girl of Ink and Stars, The* 192–195
Hoffman, M.: *Amazing Grace* 16–19
Horowitz, A.: *Grendel, The* 196–199

Ice Bear, The (Morris) 98–101; information 99; narrative 100; persuasion 101
ideas, gathering and shaping them into plan 6
immersion in text type 5
independent writing 2–7, 8–9
information(s): *Amazing Grace* (Hoffman) 16, 17; *Balaclava Story, The* (Layton) 190; *Blue Coat, The* (Lupton) 147; *Dark, The* (Snicket) 88; *Elephant's Friend, The* (Williams) 95; *Enchanted Wood, The* (Blyton) 152; *Ice Bear, The* (Morris) 99; *Legend of Podkin One-Ear, The* (Larwood) 202; *Letters from the Lighthouse* (Carroll) 181; *Mackerel and Chips* (Morpurgo) 185; *Mrs Pepperpot has a visitor from America* (Prøysen) 131; *Mrs Pepperpot's Birthday* (Prøysen) 135; *One Snowy Night* (Butterworth) 29; *Peter and the Wolf* (Prokofiev) 140; *Stick Man* (Donaldson and Scheffler) 33; *True Story of the 3 Little Pigs, The* (Scieszka) 108; *Twits, The* (Dahl) 155; *Varjak Paw* (Said) 213; *Way Back Home, The* (Jeffers) 61
information text xiii
instructions: *Ahmed and the Feather Girl* (Ray) 67; *Blue Coat, The* (Lupton) 148; *Disgusting Sandwich, The* (Edwards) 45; *Donkey Cabbage, The* (Pullman) 169; *Mr Majeika* (Carpenter) 128; *Mrs Pepperpot's Birthday* (Prøysen) 136; *Naughty Bus* (Oke and Oke) 25; *Pandora* (Turnbull) 72; *Quest* (Becker) 76; *Stick Man* (Donaldson and Scheffler) 34; *Tale of Despereaux, The* (DiCamillo) 206; *Tear Thief, The* (Duffy and Ceccoli) 54; *Twits, The* (Dahl) 156
invitation and menu: *Tiger Who Came to Tea, The* (Kerr) 57

Jeffers, O. 8; *Day the Crayons Quit, The* 40–43; *Way Back Home, The* 60–63
Journey (Becker) 20–23; explanation 21; narrative 22; recount 23

Kerr, J.: *Tiger Who Came to Tea, The* 56–59
knowledge: of child xi–xii, *xii*; combined *xii*; of pedagogy xi

Larwood, K.: *Legend of Podkin One-Ear, The* 200–203
Layton, G.: *Balaclava Story, The* 188–191
learning 2
Legend of Podkin One-Ear, The (Larwood) 200–203; information 202; narrative 203; recount 201

Letters from the Lighthouse (Carroll) 180–183; information 181; narrative 182; recount 183
letter writing 8
Lighthouse Keeper's Lunch, The (Armitage and Armitage) 48–51; descriptions 49; explanation 50; narrative 51
Lion at School (Pearce) 118–121; description 119; explanation 120; narrative 121
Little Lord Feather-Frock (Lupton) 122–125; narrative 123; persuasion 124; recount 125
long sentences xii
Lupton, H.: *Blue Coat, The* 146–149; *Little Lord Feather-Frock* 122–125

Mackerel and Chips (Morpurgo) 184–187; information 185; narrative 186; persuasion 187
mapping/story map/story board 12
Martin, A. 5
model text 8
Morpurgo, M.: *Mackerel and Chips* 184–187
Morris, J.: *Ice Bear, The* 98–101
Mr Majeika (Carpenter) 126–129; explanation 127; instructions 128; narrative 129
Mrs Pepperpot has a visitor from America (Prøysen) 130–133; information 131; narrative 132; persuasion 133
Mrs Pepperpot's Birthday (Prøysen) 134–137; information 135; instructions 136; narrative 137

narrative: *Ahmed and the Feather Girl* (Ray) 68; *Amazing Grace* (Hoffman) 16, 18; *Balaclava Story, The* (Layton) 191; *Blue Coat, The* (Lupton) 149; *Brave Little Tailor, The* (Pullman) 163; *Cogheart* (Bunzl) 167; *Dark, The* (Snicket) 89; *Day the Crayons Quit, The* (Daywalt and Jeffers) 41; *Disgusting Sandwich, The* (Edwards) 46; *Donkey Cabbage, The* (Pullman) 170; *Egg, The* (Robertson) 92; *Elephant's Friend, The* (Williams) 96; *Enchanted Wood, The* (Blyton) 153; *Fireweed* (Walsh) 174; *Girl of Ink and Stars, The* (Hargrave) 193; *Grandpa's Story* (Tan) 177; *Great Sharp Scissors* (Pearce) 115; *Grendel, The* (Horowitz) 199; *Ice Bear, The* (Morris) 100; *Journey* (Becker) 22; *Legend of Podkin One-Ear, The* (Larwood) 203; *Letters from the Lighthouse* (Carroll) 182; *Lighthouse Keeper's Lunch, The* (Armitage and Armitage) 51; *Lion at School* (Pearce) 121; *Little Lord Feather-Frock* (Lupton) 123; *Mackerel and Chips* (Morpurgo) 186; *Mr Majeika* (Carpenter) 129; *Mrs Pepperpot has a visitor from America* (Prøysen) 132; *Mrs Pepperpot's Birthday* (Prøysen) 137; *Naughty Bus* (Oke and Oke) 26; *One Snowy Night* (Butterworth) 30; *Pandora* (Turnbull) 73; *Peter and the Wolf* (Prokofiev) 141; *Quest* (Becker) 77; *Rumpelstiltskin* (Pullman) 143; *Sir Lancelot's First Quest* (Williams) 80; *Stick Man* (Donaldson and Scheffler) 35; *Storm Whale* (Brennan) 85; *Tad* (Davies) 39; *Tale of Despereaux, The* (DiCamillo) 207; *Tear Thief, The* (Duffy and Ceccoli) 55; *Tiger Who Came to Tea, The* (Kerr) 58; *Tin Forest, The* (Ward and Anderson) 103; *True Story of the 3 Little Pigs, The* (Scieszka) 109; *Twits, The* (Dahl) 157; *Undertow* (Tan) 210; *Varjak Paw* (Said) 214; *Way Back Home, The* (Jeffers) 62; writing 8–9
National Curriculum in England (2013) 7
Naughty Bus (Oke and Oke) 24–27; instructions 25; narrative 26; persuasion 27
news reports: *Ahmed and the Feather Girl* (Ray) 69; *Girl of Ink and Stars, The* (Hargrave) 195; *Undertow* (Tan) 211
non-fiction assessment xiii
novels 12; *Cogheart* (Bunzl) 164–167; *Enchanted Wood, The* (Blyton) 150–153; *Fireweed* (Walsh) 172–175; *Girl of Ink and Stars, The* (Hargrave) 192–195; *Legend of Podkin One-Ear, The* (Larwood) 200–203; *Letters from the Lighthouse* (Carroll) 180–183; *Mr Majeika* (Carpenter) 126–129; *Tale of Despereaux, The* (DiCamillo) 204–207; *Twits, The* (Dahl) 154–157; *Varjak Paw* (Said) 212–215

Oke, J.: *Naughty Bus* 24–27
One Snowy Night (Butterworth) 28–31; information 29; narrative 30; recount 31
orally rehearse 12

Pandora (Turnbull) 70–73; instruction 72; narrative 73; setting descriptions 71
paragraphs xiii
Parietti, K. 8
Pearce, P.: *Great Sharp Scissors* 114–117; *Lion at School* 118–121
personalise learning *xii*
persuasion: *Amazing Grace* (Hoffman) 16, 19; *Donkey Cabbage, The* (Pullman) 171; *Elephant's Friend, The* (Williams) 97; *Girl of Ink and Stars, The* (Hargrave) 194; *Grandpa's Story* (Tan) 178; *Great Sharp Scissors* (Pearce) 116; *Ice Bear, The* (Morris) 101; *Little Lord Feather-Frock* (Lupton) 124; *Mackerel and Chips* (Morpurgo) 187; *Mrs Pepperpot has a visitor from America* (Prøysen) 133; *Naughty Bus* (Oke and Oke) 27; *Rumpelstiltskin* (Pullman) 145; *Sir Lancelot's First Quest* (Williams) 81; *Tin Forest, The* (Ward and Anderson) 104; *Varjak Paw* (Said) 215; *Way Back Home, The* (Jeffers) 63

Peter and the Wolf (Prokofiev) 138–141; explanation 139; information 140; narrative 141
picture books: *Ahmed and the Feather Girl* (Ray) 66–69; *Amazing Grace* (Hoffman) 16–19; *Dark, The* (Snicket) 86–89; *Day the Crayons Quit, The* (Daywalt and Jeffers) 40–43; *Disgusting Sandwich, The* (Edwards) 44–47; *Egg, The* (Robertson) 90–93; *Elephant's Friend, The* (Williams) 94–97; *Ice Bear, The* (Morris) 98–101; *Journey* (Becker) 20–23; *Lighthouse Keeper's Lunch, The* (Armitage and Armitage) 48–51; *Naughty Bus* (Oke and Oke) 24–27; *One Snowy Night* (Butterworth) 28–31; *Pandora* (Turnbull) 70–73; *Quest* (Becker) 74–77; *Sir Lancelot's First Quest* (Williams) 78–81; *Stick Man* (Donaldson and Scheffler) 32–35; *Storm Whale* (Brennan) 82–85; *Tad* (Davies) 36–39; *Tear Thief, The* (Duffy and Ceccoli) 52–55; *Tiger Who Came to Tea, The* (Kerr) 56–59; *Tin Forest, The* (Ward and Anderson) 102–105; *True Story of the 3 Little Pigs, The* (Scieszka) 106–109; *Way Back Home, The* (Jeffers) 60–63
powerful texts 8
Primary National Strategies (PNS) 1
Prokofiev, S.: *Peter and the Wolf* 138–141
Prøysen, A.: *Mrs Pepperpot has a visitor from America* 130–133; *Mrs Pepperpot's Birthday* 134–137
Pullman, P.: *Brave Little Tailor, The* 160–163; *Donkey Cabbage, The* 168–171; *Rumpelstiltskin* 142–145

Quest (Becker) 74–77; explanations 75; instruction 76; narrative 77

Raising Boys' Achievements in Writing (Bearne) 1
Ray, J.: *Ahmed and the Feather Girl* 66–69
Reader in the Writer, The (Barrs and Cork) 8
reader response 11
reading: shared 5
Really Useful Literacy Book, The (Martin) 5
recount: *Amazing Grace* (Hoffman) 16; *Day the Crayons Quit, The* (Daywalt and Jeffers) 43; *Disgusting Sandwich, The* (Edwards) 47; *Egg, The* (Robertson) 93; *Fireweed* (Walsh) 175; *Grandpa's Story* (Tan) 179; *Great Sharp Scissors* (Pearce) 117; *Journey* (Becker) 23; *Legend of Podkin One-Ear, The* (Larwood) 201; *Letters from the Lighthouse* (Carroll) 183; *Little Lord Feather-Frock* (Lupton) 125; *One Snowy Night* (Butterworth) 31; *Rumpelstiltskin* (Pullman) 144; *Tiger Who Came to Tea, The* (Kerr) 59; *Tin Forest, The* (Ward and Anderson) 105
Robertson, M. P.: *Egg, The* 90–93

robust assessments xiii
Rumpelstiltskin (Pullman) 142–145; narrative 143; persuasion 145; recount 144

Said, S. F.: *Varjak Paw* 212–215
Scheffler, A.: *Stick Man* 32–35
Scieszka, J.: *True Story of the 3 Little Pigs, The* 106–109
shared reading 5
shared writing 6–8
Shaw, H.: *Disgusting Sandwich, The* 44–47
short stories 8, 12; *Balaclava Story, The* (Layton) 188–191; *Blue Coat, The* (Lupton) 146–149; *Brave Little Tailor, The* (Pullman) 160–163; *Donkey Cabbage, The* (Pullman) 168–171; *Grandpa's Story* (Tan) 176–179; *Great Sharp Scissors* (Pearce) 114–117; *Grendel, The* (Horowitz) 196–199; *Lion at School* (Pearce) 118–121; *Little Lord Feather-Frock* (Lupton) 122–125; *Mackerel and Chips* (Morpurgo) 184–187; *Mrs Pepperpot has a visitor from America* (Prøysen) 130–133; *Mrs Pepperpot's Birthday* (Prøysen) 134–137; *Peter and the Wolf* (Prokofiev) 138–141; *Rumpelstiltskin* (Pullman) 142–145; *Undertow* (Tan) 208–211
short writing 7
Sir Lancelot's First Quest (Williams) 78–81; discussion 79; narrative 80; persuasion 81
Snicket, L.: *Dark, The* 86–89
Stick Man (Donaldson and Scheffler) 32–35; information 33; instructions 34; narrative 35
Storm Whale (Brennan) 82–85; description 83; discussion 84; narrative 85
story mountain 12
success criteria 5
summative assessments xi, xiii
supported composition 6

Tad (Davies) 36–39; description 37; explanation 38; narrative 39
Tale of Despereaux, The (DiCamillo) 204–207; discussion 205; instructions 206; narrative 207
talk/word/language games 12
Tan, S.: *Grandpa's Story* 176–179; *Undertow* 208–211
teacher's knowledge of the pupils' learning xi
Teaching Sequence for Writing 3–4; extended write/completion of whole text 6–7; gathering ideas and shaping them into plan 6; immersion in text type 5
Tear Thief, The (Duffy and Ceccoli) 52–55; description 53; instructions 54; narrative 55
text: extended write/completion of 6–7; information xiii; powerful 8; structure xiii; structure target xiii

text type 4, 9, 11–12, xii, xiii, xiv; familiarising with 1, 5; immersion in 5
Tiger Who Came to Tea, The (Kerr) 56–59; invitation and menu 57; narrative 58; recount 59
Tin Forest, The (Ward and Anderson) 102–105; narrative 103; persuasion 104; recount 105
True Story of the 3 Little Pigs, The (Scieszka) 106–109; discussion 107; information 108; narrative 109
Turnbull, V.: *Pandora* 70–73
Twits, The (Dahl) 154–157; information 155; instructions 156; narrative 157

Undertow (Tan) 208–211; explanation 209; narrative 210; news report 211

Varjak Paw (Said) 212–215; information 213; narrative 214; persuassion 215

Walsh, J. P.: *Fireweed* 172–175
Ward, H.: *Tin Forest, The* 102–105
Way Back Home, The (Jeffers) 60–63; information 61; narrative 62; persuasion 63
Wiesner, D. 8
Williams, M.: *Elephant's Friend, The* 94–97; *Sir Lancelot's First Quest* 78–81
writer's hints 12
writing: baseline xiii; benefits of 7; better quality 2; curriculum 3, xiii; gaps in xiii; generic skills xiii; guided 7; independent 2–7, 8–9; letter 8; narrative 8–9; non-fiction assessment xiii; opportunities xii; shared 6–8